Type Companion
for the Digital Artist

Upper Saddle River, NJ 07458

Library of Congress Cataloging-in-Publication Data

Type companion for the digital artist
        p. cm. — (Against the Clock series)
    ISBN 0-13-040993-6

Editor-in-Chief: Stephen Helba
Director of Production and Manufacturing: Bruce Johnson
Executive Editor: Elizabeth Sugg
Managing Editor-Editorial: Judy Casillo
Editorial Assistant: Anita Rhodes
Managing Editor-Production: Mary Carnis
Production Editor: Denise Brown
Composition: Against the Clock, Inc.
Design Director: Cheryl Asherman
Senior Design Coordinator: Miguel Ortiz
Cover Design: LaFortezza Design Group, Inc.
Interior Design: Lee Goldstein
Printer/Binder: RR Donnelley & Sons

Pearson Education LTD.
Pearson Education Australia PTY, Limited
Pearson Education Singapore, Pte. Ltd
Pearson Education North Asia Ltd
Pearson Education Canada, Ltd.
Pearson Educación de Mexico, S.A. de C.V.
Pearson Education — Japan
Pearson Education Malaysia, Pte. Ltd
Pearson Education, Upper Saddle River, New Jersey

10 9 8 7 6 5 4 3 2 1

ISBN 0-13-040993-6

Contents

Preface   **vii**

INTRODUCTION   **1**

For Whom Did We Write this Book?.. 1
How Is this Book Organized?... 2
How Should I Use this Book? 3
Are You Ready to Start Exploring Type and Typography? 4

The History and Foundations of Type   **5**

1 THE EVOLUTION OF TYPOGRAPHY   **7**

The Alphabet Develops 7
    Pictographic and Syllabic Forms 7
    Phoenician Syllabic Writing 8
    Greek Development of the Alphabet 9
    The Latin Alphabet Evolves 10
Document Format Development 11
Producing Books in the Middle Ages 12
Typography and Printing Become Automated 14
The Microcomputer Impacts the Industry 17
    Publishing Beyond Paper 18
Fonts Used for Publishing 20
Summary 22
Endnote 22

2 TYPE BASICS   **23**

Analyzing Letterforms 24
    Glyph Anatomy 24
    Measuring Type 27
Font Basics 29
Dos and Don'ts 31
Summary 33

3 EXPLORING CATEGORIES OF TYPE   35

Categorizing Type 35
Evolution of Type Styles 37
    Blackletter 37
    Oldstyle 38
    Transitional 40
    Modern 41
    Slab Serif 43
    Sans Serif 46
    Script, Cursive, and Brush 47
    Decorative/Display 49
    Pi 51
Character Sets 52
    Expert Character Sets 52
Summary 53

Typography   55

4 UNDERSTANDING THE ELEMENTS OF TYPE   57

The Readability of Type 58
    Serif vs. Sans-Serif Type 58
    Weight 59
    Case 60
    Italics 61
    Measuring Type 62
        Leading 65
        Line Length 67
    Justification (Alignment) 69
    Margins and Columns 70
        Columns Per Page 72
    Color 72
    Black, White and Gray Type 75
    Tracking and Kerning 76
Special Characters 78
    Quotes and Related Characters 78
    Hyphens and Dashes 79
    Special Characters 80
    Spacing Options 81
Combining Type with Rules 81
    Rules in Columns and Tables 81
    Rules as Accents 83
Creating Lists 85
    Bulleted Lists 85
    Numbered Lists 87
    Unnumbered Lists 87
Summary 88

5 CONTROLLING TYPE WITHIN DOCUMENTS   89

Styled Type vs. Type Styles 89
Hyphenation and Justification 91
    Auto vs. Manual Hyphenation 93
    Reworking "Rivers" of Type in a Column 95
Horizontal and Vertical Alignment 96
Widow & Orphan Control 99
Working with Styles 100
    Interaction of Styles 101
Summary 103

Real-World Challenges   105

6 DESIGNING WITH TYPE   107

Matching Type to the Message 107
    Type Denotation and Connotation 108
Display Type 113
    Using Type for Headlines 114
    Type in Boxes 117
    Posters and Ads 118
    Drop Caps 119
Body Type 120
Type and Color 122
Designing Logotypes 122
Interaction of Type and Graphics 123
    Knocking Type Out of Photographs 123
    Unique Treatments of Display Type 124
    Working with Wraparounds 125
Type and the Design Grid 127
Summary 128

7 TYPE AND THE INTERNET   129

Displaying Type on Web Pages 129
Type Elements You Can't Control 131
    Default Font Size. 131
    Default Font Face 132
    Screen Resolution 133
Comparing Web and Print Documents 133
    The Fold 134
    Contrast 135
    Underlining 136
    Anti-aliasing 137

Fonts and Font Specification 138
   Microsoft Core Fonts for the Web 139
   Specifying Type in HTML 140
      Specifying Face 140
      Specifying Color 141
      Using Special Characters 142
      Headings 145
Styles 146
   Types of Styles 147
      HTML Styles 147
      Cascading Style Sheets, or CSS 148
Fonts Embedded in Documents 148
Summary 149

8 THE MECHANICS OF TYPE   **151**

Fonts in Common Use 151
   PostScript Fonts 152
      Multiple Master Fonts 153
   TrueType 153
   Open Type 154
Naming Fonts 154
Font Matching 156
Managing Fonts on the Computer 158
Managing Fonts for Printing 160
   Font-Related Printing Problems 161
      Printing Tricks 162
      VMError 162
      Nostringval or Typecheck 162
      LimitCheck 162
      RangeCheck/SetPageParam 163
      Dicstack Overflow 163
      −8133 (Macintosh Only) 163
      Undefined Offending Command: [various] 163
Summary 164

LAST THOUGHTS   **165**

Gallery & Reference   **167**

    GALLERY   **169**

    GLOSSARY   **181**

    INDEX   **197**

Preface

The *Against The Clock Companion Series* offers insight into fundamental artistic issues. It covers the details of broad design topics such as:

The basic rules of good design,

The proper and effective use of color,

The history and application of typography,

Typography's role in the design process,

The principles underlying proven and compelling Web-site design.

The *Against The Clock Companion Series* works together with application-specific libraries of training and skills-development books. The books in the series provide background in fundamental design and artistic issues. They complement the hands-on, skills-based approach of the *Against the Clock* and other applications titles. The series:

Contains **richly illustrated, real-world examples** of commercial and institutional artwork, designs, packaging and other creative assignments;

Provides the reasoning behind the **creative strategies, production methodologies and distribution models** — in the words of the artists who provided them;

Addresses the four most important disciplines critical to successful use of computer arts applications: **design, color, typography and Web-page design**;

Presents the material in a **friendly and easy-to-understand** manner, rather than relying on technical jargon or obsolete terminology.

The books in the Companion Series are:

Design Companion for the Digital Artist (ISBN: 0-13-091237-9)

Typography Companion for the Digital Artist (ISBN: 0-13-040993-6)

Web Design Companion for the Digital Artist (ISBN: 0-13-097355-6)

Color Companion for the Digital Artist (ISBN: 0-13-097524-9)

We hope that you'll find the books as effective and useful as we found them exciting and fun to develop. As always, we welcome any comments you might have that will make the next editions of the books even better. Please feel free to contact us at computer_arts@prenhall.com.

About Against The Clock

Against The Clock (ATC) was founded in 1990 and went on to become one of the nation's leading systems integration and training firms. The organization, founded by Ellenn Behoriam, specialized in developing custom training materials for clients such as L.L. Bean, *The New England Journal of Medicine*, the Smithsonian, the National Education Association, *Air & Space Magazine*, Publishers Clearing House, the National Wildlife Society, Home Shopping Network and many others.

Building on their lengthy experience creating focused and structured training materials, ATC's management team began working with major publishers in the mid-nineties to produce high-quality application and workflow-specific training aids. In 1996, ATC introduced the highly popular "Creative Techniques" series, which focused on real-world examples of award-winning commercial design, imaging and Web-page development. Working with Adobe Press, they also developed successful management books, including *Workflow Reengineering*, which won the IDIA award as most effective book of the year in 1997.

In 1998, the company entered into a long-term relationship with Prentice Hall/Pearson Education. This relationship allows ATC to focus on bringing high-quality content to the marketplace to address up-to-the-minute software releases. The Against The Clock library has grown to include over 35 titles — focusing on all aspects of computer arts. From illustration to Web-site design, from image to animation, and from page layout to effective production techniques, the series is highly regarded and is recognized as one of the most powerful teaching and training tools in the industry.

Against The Clock, Inc. is located in Tampa, Florida and can be found on the Web at www.againsttheclock.com.

About the Author

Robin McAllister is a writer educator, and consultant to the graphic arts industry. He has been speaking about and teaching others to create effective pages and to manage their graphics businesses since the early 1980s. In the process of teaching others, he's written many "how to" guides and training manuals. Rob is a contributing editor for Hayden Books' *FreeHand Graphics Studio Skills,* and is the author of a Delmar Publishers' *Pathways to Print* series.

Rob is the team leader for America Online's Applied Computing Community. He is also a technical editor for *Electronic Publishing*, a contributing editor for *Printing News* and senior project manager for Against The Clock.

Acknowledgments

I would like to thank the writers, editors, illustrators and production staff who have worked long and hard to complete the Against The Clock series.

Thank you to our technical team of teaching professionals whose comments and expertise contributed to the success of this book, including Doris Anton, Wichita Area Technical College; Dee A. Colvin, University of North Florida; Carin Murphy; Des Moines Area Technical College; Sherri Hill, Manatee Community College; John Luttropp, Montclair State University; James Wiese, Columbus College of Art and Design; and Ken Botnick, Washington University-St. Louis.

A big thank you to all of the artists who contributed their work in the gallery and throughout this book.

Thanks to Terry Sisk Graybill, senior editor and final link in the chain of production, for her tremendous help in making sure we all said what we meant to say.

Thank you to Judy Casillo, Developmental Editor, and Denise Brown, Production Editor, for their guidance, patience and attention to detail.

Introduction

To the making of books there is no end.
—SOLOMON

There are hundreds, even thousands of books about typography available, not to mention the chapters on the subject in books about design and printing. So, why create yet another book to fill up the shelf?

Much as we would like to write "The Definitive Tome about Type and Typography," this will never happen. Why? Because, along with the rest of the graphic-arts industry, typography is constantly evolving. Because much of the "factual" information contradicts other "factual" information. Because there are a variety of ways of achieving typographic goals. Because typography is subjective — in a room full of 12 designers, you will probably have 24 conflicting opinions about type.

What we have produced — we hope — is a useful companion book to the step-by-step books that are *Against the Clock's* core publications, or with other publications that may be used as core teaching material. Our goal in producing this typography companion work was to deliver an overview of the rich history of typography and to help you produce better typography through an understanding of its principles, of the mechanics of the software programs you use and of the type itself.

For Whom Did We Write this Book?

Perhaps the hardest job facing us, as we began the process of writing, was identifying our target audience. We did not write specifically to the design professional or fine-arts major. Nor did we direct the material to those who primarily use word processors, which do not have the controls necessary to effect many typographic nuances. Both of these groups, we believe, can benefit from much of the material in this book. We have, however, directed this information to the graphic artist, the desktop publisher, the person who lives in the hands-on world of printing and publishing every day.

We believe that graphic arts professionals (and those aspiring to become such) will gain the most from our discussions. It has been our intention to build appreciation for the heritage that is typography, and to help you understand the nuts and bolts of the type that we use in our documents. We want you use the book as a reference, so when you learn how to build a style sheet in a DTP program, or how to create cascading style sheets in a Web-page creation program, you have a solid foundation upon which to base your new knowledge.

Unlike Against the Clock's core publications, this companion book is not filled with exercises, nor does it give you specific projects on which to work. It does, however, give you many suggestions that you can put to work immediately, and suggests ways in which you can expand your typographic horizons.

How Is this Book Organized?

We begin at the beginning. Section 1, *The History and Foundations of Type*, includes Chapters 1 through 3. It begins with an historical overview, takes you through the development of letterform and concludes with a discussion of the categories of type.

Chapter 1, *The Evolution of Typography*, discusses the development of the Latin alphabet and the development of documents, including media and production methods. We also discuss the automation of printing and typography, and explore the effects of technology, especially in the 20th century.

Chapter 2, *Type Basics*, helps you analyze the letterform, beginning with learning the parts of letters. You learn to measure type, both horizontally and vertically. You learn some font basics, including differences between fonts in a Windows environment and fonts in a Macintosh environment. We conclude with some Dos and Don'ts.

We immerse ourselves in *Exploring the Categories of Type* in Chapter 3. After discussing some specific categorization systems, we learn how type is categorized, using an illustrated history of representative typefaces. Finally, we look at the contents of nonstandard character sets.

Section 2, *Typography*, moves away from the physical aspects of type and toward composition techniques for creating attractive, effective documents.

In Chapter 4, *Understanding the Elements of Type*, we discuss the aspects of type and typography, with the goal of producing type that is highly readable. We explore how type is specified and controlled within publishing programs. In this chapter, we learn to use special characters correctly, spurning a typewritten look in favor of a more professional look using typographic characters. In addition, we learn to combine rules (lines) with type, both to better define pages and to create more compelling imagery.

We build upon our knowledge in Chapter 5, *Controlling Type within Documents*. We learn to apply automatic functions of publishing programs in order to achieve typographic excellence with a minimum of manual intervention. We learn to get the most from hyphenation and justification routines, how to achieve effective vertical alignment, and how to control widows and orphans in documents. Finally, we investigate the power of style sheets.

Our third section, *Real-world Challenges*, digs into the opportunities associated with designing for print and for electronic distribution.

It is in Chapter 6, *Designing with Type*, that we show you what to look for to get the "right look" from the typefaces you use. We first discuss matching type to the message, and proceed to a discussion of display type as it is used in headlines, in posters and in ads. We help you decide how to select body type, keeping the physical structure of the publication and the needs of the audience in mind. Finally, we consider logotypes and the interaction of type and graphics.

The challenges and opportunities of *Type and the Internet* are the subjects considered in Chapter 7. First, we generally discuss the challenge to designers presented by the Web. We proceed into the solution suggested by Cascading Style Sheets, including the hierarchy of style sheets, concepts of style-sheet design, and a discussion of font and text properties. The chapter concludes as we explore the solutions offered by Embedded Open Type and TrueDoc.

You might call Chapter 8, *The Mechanics of Type*, the nuts-and-bolts chapter of this book. Here we delve into the computer code that makes up typefaces to see what makes them tick. We then explore font-matching conventions, and discuss how to manage fonts on the computer and in the print stream, concluding with some troubleshooting solutions.

How Should I Use this Book?

We hope that you'll read through the first few chapters, and then pick up magazines and other documents to see how others apply this information. You might next sit down at your computer, with your favorite publishing program open in front of you, and try out a few "what ifs" of your own, as you apply the information in later chapters.

As you read through Chapter 3, you might want to look through magazines with good typography and lots of ads, then see how comprehensive your analysis of letterforms is. See if you can categorize type that you find in publications according to the categorization system we show you — there's a good chance you'll end up fairly impressed with yourself.

When you've completed Chapter 4, you might go to your magazines and dissect the typography. What's good? What's bad? How could the information you now have be used to improve the bad type? (Remember not to be *too* subjective about good vs. bad type.)

Chapter 5 is particularly useful while your publishing program is running. See if you can become comfortable with the typographic controls that your program gives you. If you're having a problem, and you have ATC courseware handy, pull out the courseware. Otherwise, grab your manual and take control of your type.

After completing Chapter 6, it's time to find some examples of where type was well matched to the message, and some examples where it wasn't. Get examples of good and bad headlines, and start a collection of logotypes. (You may want to make this an ongoing project — logotypes you collect may inspire you in an upcoming design job.) Find some examples of unique treatment of headlines, and some good and bad samples of type interacting with graphics.

Chapter 7 gives you the opportunity to surf the net looking for good applications of text. Be sure to use the Source view in your browser to discover how others use fonts and style sheets effectively on their Web sites. Bookmark the good ones for reference. If you're up to it, try creating your own Web pages using cascading style sheets, or download WEFT from Microsoft and try your hand at font embedding.

When you're done with Chapter 8, you should have a good idea as to how you want to manage fonts on your computer. Dig in and put your new management skills to use.

Are You Ready to Start Exploring Type and Typography?

Then jump right in. We hope you enjoy reading and working with this publication as much as we enjoyed collecting the information and putting it together!

SECTION 1

THE HISTORY AND FOUNDATIONS OF TYPE

*To give an accurate description of what never happened
is the proper occupation of the historian.*

— OSCAR WILDE

Any time a history is written — particularly one covering a multitude of events and time periods — the writer is bound to tread upon the well-entrenched beliefs of a number of readers and bolster the predisposition of others. So it is with history.

As you skim through thousands of years of recorded history, you will note how the development of our alphabet and basic document technologies are compressed into a relatively narrow time period. Automation of the printing and publishing process is really quite recent — occupying a scant 600 years — and so much has occurred in the last century!

A result of the evolution of typography and finally the revolution that began in the last quarter of the 20th century has been the decline and fall of typographic expertise. While today we have more typefaces than ever before — and they are being created at an ever-increasing rate — we have lost nuances of craftsmanship because typography is too often treated as a commodity instead of a craft.

We return to some of the basics, bearing in mind that type is properly part of a document's design; but even more important is the message that the type allows us to read. Both the art of typeface design and the art of presenting text are important. When we analyze letterforms, we are interested in being able to identify parts of letters, but more to the point, we are then able to speak intelligently with other designers and typographers about the characteristics of specific typefaces.

Nuances such as specifying type have become foreign to designers since the introduction of desktop publishing in the mid-1980s, because it has become so easy to simply resize the type. Measuring type horizontally and vertically is a mechanical skill that — once you have mastered it — achieves the level of an art.

It is equally important to learn differences between typefaces on Windows-based computers and on Macintoshes. When the differences are known and acknowledged, cross-platform problems, such as unwanted font substitution, can be alleviated or avoided altogether. Since the computer is not a typewriter, it needs to be used differently. We will help you understand some of the differences, so you'll produce better documents in a shorter period of time.

As you will see, categorizing type, learning about typefaces within specific type categories, and gaining some anecdotal information about some type designers can be both fun and informative. You will discover how to categorize type, and learn about non-standard character sets that add to the typographic beauty of your documents.

When you have completed this section, you should understand how language, alphabets and type evolved, and some of the reasons for the evolution. You should have some idea of the challenges that lie ahead. In addition, you will have explored the makeup of individual type characters and know the characteristics of classes of type, using the Lawson system of categorization.

CHAPTER 1

The Evolution of Typography

Typography has been described as a merging of art and science. The art of typography is readily visible, but its science lies beneath the surface. In this chapter, we will explore the development of type as it relates to the publishing process. We will discuss type categorization in Chapter 3 and the mechanics of type in Chapter 8.

The science of typography has evolved along with the technology used to publish documents. Whatever forms the written word has taken through the millennia have been driven by our desire to communicate better and more efficiently with one another.

Before the development of the letterform, however, came the initial development of written language. Our Western alphabet followed a path that was millennia in the making.

The Alphabet Develops

Presumably the first meaningful human communication was speech. Since speech required that individuals be near one another, other mechanisms were needed to permit accurate communications at a distance, or over time (even with future generations). As we explore the evolution of communication, we note the related finds of archaeological excavations, which have uncovered such items as monumental wall paintings and inscriptions on pottery discussing daily life.

Pictographic and Syllabic Forms

Many of the older forms of picture writing were highly detailed works of art, illustrating a specific event. As it became important to communicate more generically, the symbols were simplified and standardized. Egyptian hieroglyphs and Chinese ideograms are early forms of this picture writing.

There were really two kinds of writing for the Egyptians: word-signs, or logograms, and syllabic signs. We use similar word-signs today, such as "&" for "and," "$" for "dollars" and "=" for "equals." While modern English has a sound for each letter, the ancients had a sound for each syllable, or sometimes for multiple syllables. Consequently there were hundreds of syllabic signs.

Standardized symbols allow us a look at ancient Egyptian culture, through a study of their hieroglyphic writings.

Another pictographic writing system was cuneiform writing. The word "cuneiform" is from a Latin word meaning "wedge-shaped." Figures were pressed into soft clay tablets with the slanted edge of a stylus, giving them a unique wedge shape. Cuneiform was not a language, but a set of symbols that gained almost universal acceptance in the Middle East. The oldest dated cuneiform tablet, from the Sumerian city of Unik (Erech), is from 3100 BCE. This form of writing was passed from one culture to another and predominated through the fall of the Babylonian empire in the 6th century BCE.*

Between 1500 and 1000 BCE, the Semites of Syria and other parts of the Middle East created their own system of writing based on the Egyptian syllabic signs. They discarded all of the multi-consonant signs and created a new syllabary of about 30 signs, each consisting of one consonant plus any vowel. While these early systems died out, they may have influenced the syllabic writing form that spread through the world.

A syllabary is a list of symbols, each of which represents a syllable.

Phoenician Syllabic Writing

From the Phoenician city of Byblos, already famous for exporting the writing material papyrus, came a new syllabic writing style, consisting of only 22 signs (all consonants). The reader filled in the vowels, based on structure and context, so *wndr* could be understood to be *wonder* or *wander*. While this seems awkward, we can illustrate that such a structure is not all that difficult. Test yourself:

Y cn prbly rd ths sntnc.

*The abbreviation BCE (Before the Common Era) and CE (Common Era) are preferred to the more common BC (Before Christ) and AD (Anno Domini — In the Year of Our Lord) in deference to those whose religion is not Christian.

Because the Phoenicians were seafaring traders, they carried their writing form throughout the Mediterranean world, from Yemen to Ethiopia, where this ancient language is still in use today.

Aramaic, which replaced the older Hebrew writing style, was an important branch of the Phoenician writing style. Much of the Bible was written in Aramaic, and this square writing style is still used today. The northern Arabs took over a form of the Aramaic system, and with the rise of Islam, spread it to the far corners of the earth.

Greek Development of the Alphabet

After about 100 years, the Greeks liberally borrowed Phoenician writing, keeping the forms, the names of the signs, the order of the signs in the alphabet and the direction of the writing (right to left). Later, the Greek form would change considerably, both in the shape of the letters and in other key structures of the writing form. Gradually the Greeks evolved a writing style with a consistent left-to-right format.

The Greeks altered the names of the Phoenician letters only slightly. Alpha, beta, gamma and delta replaced the characters aleph, beth, gimel and daleth. Three signs were dropped, and two changed their original value, namely *.t* and *.s*, which became *th* and *x*. Five new signs were added: *upsilon, phi, chi, psi* and *omega*.

Name	Character		Transliteration
Alpha	A	α	a
Beta	B	β	b
Gamma	Γ	γ	g
Delta	Δ	δ ∂[1]	d
Epsilon	E	ε	e
Zeta	Z	ζ	z
Eta	H	η	ē
Theta	Θ	θ ϑ[1]	th
Iota	I	ι	i
Kappa	K	κ	k
Lambda	Λ	λ	l
Mu	M	μ	m
Nu	N	ν	n
Xi	Ξ	ξ	x
Omicron	O	o	o
Pi	Π	π	p
Rho	P	ρ	r,[2]
Sigma	Σ	σ	s
Tau	T	τ	t
Upsilon[4]	Υ	υ	u[3]
Phi[4]	Φ	φ φ[1]	ph
Chi[4]	X	χ	kh
Psi[4]	Ψ	ψ	ps
Omega[4]	Ω	ω	ō

1. Old-style character. Usually used in math formulas. Should not be combined with other forms.

2. Pronounced rh if initial letter; when double, pronounced rrh.

3. Often y except after a, e, ē and i.

4. Greeks added these letters to the Phoenician alphabet.

The Greek alphabet, which had both consonants and vowels, is the basis of the alphabet we use today.

We illustrated earlier that reading common words without consonants is not that difficult, but in some instances, common words would not be used — as is the case with names. The Greeks systematically plugged in six signs with weak consonants — sounds that were used only in the Phoenician language and, hence, were of no use to the Greeks as consonants. They were turned into the vowels *a, e, u, E, i* and *o*. Once this was done, the remainder of the symbols were no longer needed to represent syllables, but were simply used as consonants. For the first time, an entire alphabet existed, composed of both consonants and vowels.

The Latin Alphabet Evolves

The alphabet was passed on to the Etruscans, the Copts of Egypt and the Slavonic people of Eastern Europe. Latin writing, like the earlier Greek, consisted of 24 letters, but there were significant differences. The Greek *diagamma* sign of *w* became *f*, and the Greek *eta* (h) became *h*. The Greek *gamma* for *g* was used in older Latin for both *c* and *g*, and the *g* was later differentiated from the *c* by the addition of a small horizontal bar (which we see in the English capital *G*).

Diacritical marks are accents such as the acute accent (á), grave accent (à), umlaut or diaresis (ü), circumflex (ê), tilde (ñ) and cedilla (ç).

Further development removed the letters *th, z* and *x* in early Latin writing. As you know, the *x* and *z* were later reinserted at the end of the alphabet, along with the letters *v* and *y*. In the Middle Ages, when the letters *j* and *w* were added, the Latin alphabet increased to its present size of 26 distinct letters. Sounds were further differentiated by combining letters, such as the English *sh,* or by adding diacritical marks, such as the French *ç.*

The Greeks, Romans and the people of the Near East used two forms of letter construction — carefully drawn letterform with squarish, separate signs, used on official documents and monuments, and less carefully drawn cursive writing with rounded, often joined symbols on less official documents.

A form of capital letter was introduced in the Middle Ages. Uncials (from the Latin, meaning "inch high") were squarish in shape, with rounded strokes. These letters were used in Western Europe in handwritten books, in conjunction with small-letter cursive writing.

The Uncial style was introduced in the Middle Ages.

Following the Renaissance, two types of letters were distinguished: majuscules (capital letters) and miniscules (small letters), continuing the tradition of medieval cursive writing.

Development of the Modern Alphabet

6000	5000	4000	3000	2000	1000	BCE/CE	1000	2000

Pictograms   Sumerian   Phoenician   Greek/Latin   Renaissance
Ideograms   Cuneiform   & Aramaic
Hieroglyphs

Pictographic and syllabic forms of writing were used for more than half of recorded history.

Document Format Development

Documents through the ages have taken many forms. Early permanent writings were chiseled in stone, and many of those have survived until our day. Huge slabs of stone, however, are not very portable.

Early records were scratched on bark or leather, or other moderately durable material. The Sumerians, Assyrians, Babylonians and others of the Middle East pressed their cuneiform characters into moist clay tablets. If the record was intended to become permanent, the tablet was then baked in an oven. The laws of Solon were carved into wooden tablets and set up in the Acropolis in Greece, just as the Twelve Tables of Roman law were engraved in wood.

As cultures became more dependent upon the written word, it became necessary to create documents that were more portable. The Greeks and Romans used small wax tablets for brief documents of a less-permanent nature. Small boards with narrow frames were overlaid with a thin coating of black wax, into which letters were scratched with a stylus, allowing the lighter-colored wood to show through. The tablets could be bound together with thongs or metal rings; a group of tablets bound together was called a "codex."

Longer documents were made of papyrus, a parchment-like paper made from the pith, or inner portion of the stalk, of the papyrus plant. The pith was cut into thin strips, pressed together and dried to form a smooth, thin writing surface.

The sheets of papyrus were glued together, side to side, to form a roll (scroll) 5–12 inches wide and 15–40 feet long, with writing on only one side. The roll was called a "volumen"; its papyrus was rolled around a brightly painted, gilded stick with knobs at both ends, called an "umbilicus." The roll was held in the right hand and unrolled, column by column, onto the roller held in the left hand. When the reader reached the end of the roll or had read enough, the roll was rewound onto the umbilicus. The dry air of Egypt and the desert areas of the Middle East and the cedar oil in which the papyrus was soaked have preserved papyrus rolls that are thousands of years old.

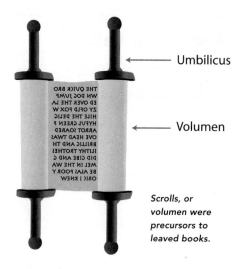

Umbilicus

Volumen

Scrolls, or volumen were precursors to leaved books.

Gradually, leaved books replaced scrolls and parchment, made from the skins of sheep and goats, replaced papyrus. Vellum, made from calfskin, was used for special copies of books. Vellum and parchment were made by carefully washing the skins, then covering them with lime to loosen the hair. When the hair was removed, the skin was stretched on a frame, scraped, dusted with sifted chalk and polished with pumice.

Parchment and vellum were used as early as the 5th century BCE. They gradually replaced papyrus, beginning about 100 CE, and virtually displacing papyrus by the middle of the 5th century as the standard material for a book or codex. The sheets were cut to a uniform size and bound together on one side with leather thongs.

Far to the east, the Chinese developed the art of papermaking. The Arabs learned the art from them and introduced paper into Europe in the 12th century CE, after which Europeans developed their own papermaking methods. The first European papermill was built in 1270 CE in Fabriano, Italy.

Paper was first made by the Chinese in individual sheets. A pulp made up of fibers from rags and plants was mixed with water. When a sheet mold was immersed in the pulp, the fibers interlocked. The mold was removed and set aside to dry.

Producing Books in the Middle Ages

For practically a thousand years after the fall of Rome, all books were written by hand, one character at a time, using pens made from a reed or a quill from the wing of a large bird. The pens were cut with a broad end, or nib, shaped like a chisel. As a result, when the pen was used to draw a vertical stroke, the stroke was broad; horizontal strokes used the narrow edge of the pen. A curved letter had thick and thin strokes, dependent upon the angle at which the quill was held.

The ink used for writing on vellum, and later on paper, was either lampblack ink, which had been developed for use with papyrus, or an ink made from iron filings and oak bark, boiled in vinegar and bound to the vellum with gum arabic. The scribe ruled the page, marked margins and drew nearly invisible guidelines.

> *You might think of the scriptorium as a modern print shop or ad agency. Each person had a specific job or responsibility: lay out the book, ink the pages, proofread to ensure an error-free result, color the illustrations and add gold leaf to special pages.*

Most manuscripts produced in this era were the work of monks. In some monasteries, each monk worked at his own desk in a large room called the "scriptorium." In other monasteries, especially in the early part of the Middle Ages, each monk worked in his own cell.

Around 1200 CE, secular scribes also entered book production, producing texts required for university courses. Books were rented to students and teachers by book dealers known as "stationers"; when the student left the university for any reason, the book was turned back to the stationers; it was a crime to remove books. As universities grew in size, the stationers would sell their texts instead of renting them, with a change in name to *librarian*. The booksellers were considered professionals, not ordinary tradesmen.

> *The earlier book dealers were librarians as we know the word today; they rented books and allowed students to examine them without removing them from the premises*

While in France and Italy the book trade was closely tied to the universities, in England, Germany and the Low Countries, there was trade in both scholarly and popular books, including almanacs, books on astrology, cooking and other subjects. After the introduction of paper, the cost of books was greatly reduced.

> *Modern universities developed from the European universities of the Middle Ages. The word "university," taken from the Latin universitas, implies that a university should deal with a universe of subjects — nearly all fields of learning should be taught.*

In addition to text-heavy books, small religious documents called "block books" were printed from engraved blocks of wood, which we would call "woodcuts" today. The process by which they were printed was known as "xylography." In 1438 Johannes Gutenberg became a partner in a block-printing firm. For 10 years he experimented with wood and metal type.

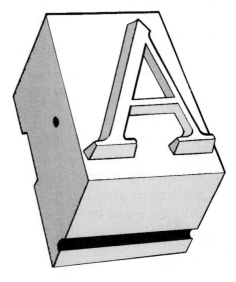

Blocks of wood were used to print publications prior to the invention of movable type.

Typography and Printing Become Automated

In 1448, Gutenberg returned to his hometown of Mainz to set up his own press. He went into partnership with a wealthy financier and his son, and set in movable type, the text for a Turkish calendar and for his masterpiece, the 42-line Bible. A year later he quarreled with his partners and lost control of his printing establishment; he was financially ruined.

> **The Gutenberg Bible, also known as the Mazarin Bible and the 42-Line Bible, was printed in Latin in Mainz, Germany, sometime between 1450 and 1456. The book is the first volume known to have been printed with movable metal type, and is Gutenberg's claim to fame. There were 42 lines of type to a page.**

Pages like this one, the first page of the Bible book of Apocalypse (Revelation), were printed on Gutenberg's and other early presses. Note the hand-inserted illuminated text.

In these few short years, Gutenberg changed the world of communications, as we know it, and made a name for himself. Because the type was movable and reusable, it became practical to make multiple copies of type-heavy documents. The written word had finally become the published (from the Latin *publicare*) word, available to the public at large.

Printers initially fashioned their documents as close as possible to the style of the manuscripts of the scribes. They used type that resembled the hand-lettered look, used the same abbreviations and special signs, and even left space for woodcut illustrations that would be hand-colored, or for hand-drawn illustrations to be inserted. While this was beautiful, it wasn't particularly easy to read, nor was it good for a fast-paced workflow.

> **Movable type was originally invented by the Chinese, around 1040. However, because their language was composed of ideograms instead of alphabetic characters, it was discarded as impractical.**

For the next 400 years, printers followed much the same process. While there were improvements in the mechanism of printing presses, letters were still set in place one by one, being assembled in a shallow hand-held tray called a "composing stick." After each line of type was spaced to fit snugly in the width allocated, a strip of lead, usually two points wide, was inserted between lines. If no lead was inserted, the type was said to be "set solid." If more than 6 points were inserted, the inserted lead was called a "slug." The type was then locked into a frame or *chase*, the type was inked, paper placed on it and an imprint was made. Majuscules were stored in the upper type case and miniscules were stored in the lower case.

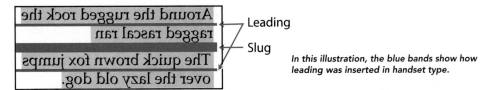

Leading

Slug

In this illustration, the blue bands show how leading was inserted in handset type.

In 1886, Ottmar Merganthaler changed the world of composition again. He developed a key-operated linesetting and typecasting machine that employed reusable brass matrices. His invention cast an entire line of type at a time; because of this, it was called the "Linotype." This was the *first generation* of automated typesetting systems. Eventually, tape drives from a variety of manufacturers would drive these machines, allowing greater productivity.

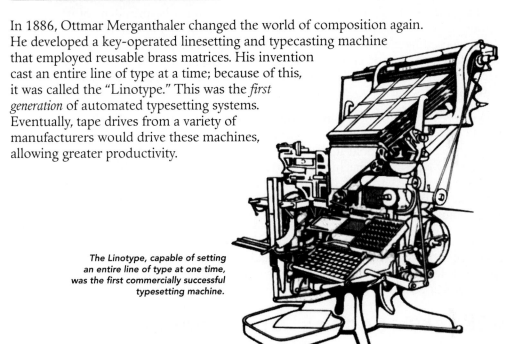

The Linotype, capable of setting an entire line of type at one time, was the first commercially successful typesetting machine.

Although Merganthaler's Linotype was the first commercially successful type-setting machine, William Church devised a typesetting machine in 1822. The Kiegl Composer (1839) and the Clay and Rosenberg Type-setter and Distributor (1840) both closely resembled upright pianos.

Unfortunately, lead is a very soft metal, and the slugs of lead would wear down quickly. To solve this problem, a means of making more durable plates was invented. The most common methods were electrotyping and stereotyping. In the electrotyping process, type is set and a cast (usually from wax) is made; it is then coated in graphite and placed in an electroplating bath. A copper shell is built up in the shape of the original type. Stereotyping begins by making a mold of the type using a heat-resistant papier-mâché. Molten metal is then poured into the mold to create the cast plate.

This process is used for *letterpress* or relief printing, where the type and any graphics are raised elements and are literally pressed onto the paper. Offset lithography, however, has been the predominant printing process since the early 1980s. The lithographic principle is that grease and water don't mix. The printing plate, made of aluminum, steel, an alloy, or a man-made material, is treated so that grease (ink) will stick to some areas and not to others. The image is offset onto a roller, and transferred to the paper. Since the process does not require a raised surface, the printing plates are made using a photographic process, either directly etched, or imaged from film, much as a black and white print would be.

To create type for this process directly requires that the type be photographically imaged to film. In the early 1950s, Varityper and Photon (the president of which later cofounded Compugraphic Corporation) each introduced a reasonably priced, stand-alone typesetting system. These were *second-generation* typesetters. They used device-dependent glass, plastic and film masters. Light was flashed through the master onto photosensitive material, which was then developed and eventually contact-printed to a printing plate.

The typefaces were provided in a variety of forms: as spinning disks, filmstrips, glass-matrix grids or disks comprised of sectors. In the early days, four typefaces (usually a plain, italic, bold and bold italic of the same family) could be accessed at any time. Some of the typesetting machines would allow type to be set only at specified sizes, and others, such as the Varityper system, used a zoom lens, allowing all point sizes within a given range to be set. Eventually some second-generation systems were expanded to allow simultaneous access to more typefaces.

These early typesetters would show the operator one or two lines of type, using a system-generated OCR-like character. In addition, there was a notation of how much space was left on each line, given in units that varied on a manufacturer-by-manufacturer basis. A common value was 18 units per em.

OCR characters are generated on low-resolution monitors.

Ugly OCR characters like this are easily generated on the low-resolution monitors used in the '70s and early '80s. You had no idea what the type would look like, but at least you could ensure that everything was spelled properly before committing a line to type.

In the 1970s, *third-generation* typesetters used electronically stored font data generated from a cathode-ray tube or laser character generator and "drawn" onto the photosensitive material. Through the early '80s, these machines were the workhorses of the printing and publishing industry. They were often configured into multi-station workgroups.

When third-generation typesetters were introduced, a passive preview was available for some models, and multiple lines of text (still OCR-like characters) could be retained on the screen. To preview your screen, it was necessary to switch from typesetting mode to preview mode, then switch back again to resume typing.

Neither second- nor third-generation typesetters could incorporate graphics more complex than horizontal or vertical rules, and even that capability was a result of their having the ruling routines stored as font data. As powerful as the computers were, it was still necessary to prepare artwork manually and combine it with the type in the final film.

> **WYSIWYG — What You See Is What You Get — is still an unrealized dream, because a monitor does not exactly replicate a printed document. What You See Is More Or Less What You Get — WYSIMOLWYG — is nearer the truth.**

Imagesetters — the *fourth generation* — also use electronically stored font data, but they have the added ability to combine line art and halftones with the type (a completely composed page). Some use dedicated front-end terminals, and others used Windows, Unix, DOS or Macintosh computers to enter the data. With the fourth generation came active preview — WYSIWYG capability.

Other than Intertype and Linotype linecaster matrices, fonts have never been interchangeable from system to system, although some second-generation and third-generation fonts would run on different models.

Every time a typesetter changed equipment, an entire type library had to be purchased anew. Even when equipment was purchased from the same manufacturer, a new library was often required. Since manufacturers of the typesetting equipment were also the type foundries, an upgrade meant substantial profits for them. Regardless of the upgrade path, every time one upgraded to a new generation of equipment, it meant also purchasing a new font library.

Because of the huge investments in equipment and in fonts (an average font cost $42 — that's $168 for a family of four fonts; ITC fonts carried an additional $30 licensing fee per font), printers, typesetting companies and some in-plant facilities owned typesetting equipment. Designers and others in the publishing business specified and ordered type.

> **ITC, the International Typeface Corporation, (later acquired by Agfa/Monotype) licenses typeface designs that meet specific criteria, including families of type in which various weights meet ITC specifications.**

The Microcomputer Impacts the Industry

In the 1950s and 1960s, computers were monster number crunchers, fed and cherished by the all-knowing custodians of Data Processing. In the 1970s, minicomputers were introduced. These machines were adapted for work in the office and in the typesetting communities. They were interactive, text-based machines. Soon after, the microcomputer evolved and was adapted for publishing.

In the late 1970s, two system standards were emerging: Apple-DOS and CP/M. IBM had yet to get involved with personal computers. August 1981 brought the IBM PC and MS-DOS into the ring. Hewlett-Packard introduced the LaserJet, bringing about a new quality level for printing and some interesting possibilities for both office and printing environments. In 1984 Apple introduced the Macintosh, which was regarded by many in the professional typesetting world as a bad joke — how could this small computer, which output ugly 300-dpi type possibly be regarded seriously, compared to their big, networked, systems?

A phenomenon was occurring in the publishing industry. With the introduction of these computers, it became possible to use off-the-shelf hardware with custom software to set type and incorporate images. Fonts were being offered by companies like Bitstream for use on multiple systems.

There was still a barrier to a seamless interface between creating documents and imaging them. Each output device required its own driver, so pages might not be correctly interpreted if they were not designed with that output device as the designated printer. What was needed was a universal interface between the front end (the screen representation of the page) and the back end (the printed page).

In 1985, events occurred that would drastically change the accepted approach to publishing and document production. Adobe Systems, of Mountain View, California, introduced the PostScript page-description language, licensing its use to any who wished to buy into the program. In a major coup, they entered into an agreement with Linotype Corporation, arguably the de facto standard for type in the United States, to digitize their very substantial library as PostScript fonts. Because PostScript was used as the device driver for both the proofing device (the laser printer) and for the imaging device, the output was consistent. Even though the laser-printer resolution was only 300 spots per inch (spi) and the imaging device had a resolution of 1270 spi, the page geometry was the same. (Spots per inch are often referred to as "dots per inch.")

> *Because of PostScript, what you proofed to your low-resolution laser printer actually showed you how the final, high-resolution document would look. This was as significant as the introduction of the Linotype.*

At approximately the same time, Aldus Corporation released PageMaker (its president, Paul Brainerd, coined the term "desktop publishing"). Apple released the LaserWriter, which used the PostScript language, and Linotype followed shortly with the L-100 imagesetter. The package of off-the-shelf hardware and software for publishing was complete.

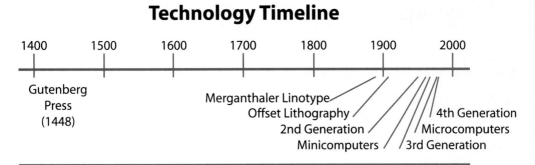

Technology Timeline

1400　1500　1600　1700　1800　1900　2000

Gutenberg
Press
(1448)

Merganthaler Linotype
Offset Lithography
2nd Generation
Minicomputers
4th Generation
Microcomputers
3rd Generation

Technology has been a contributing force to the development of publishing. Notice how rapidly the changes have come in the second half of the 20th century.

The result of these events was a paradigm shift in the cycle of document production. It became affordable for designers and corporations to perform all the typesetting and most of the composition functions of page production themselves, taking their files to a graphic arts service provider (called a "service bureau" in those early days) for imaging to film or photographic paper.

This was a devastating blow to the typesetting portion of the graphic-arts industry, forcing the closure of many shops and a downsizing of many more. Some attempted to shift gears with their clients and became service bureaus, adding high-end scanning and related equipment-dependent services that were beyond the financial means of their clients, or services that were more technical than most clients desired to perform. A few succeeded.

> *Approximately every 18 months, the capability of computers in publishing doubles. In other words, if you spend $1,000 today for publishing technology, that same investment will purchase twice the capability in a year-and-a-half.*

As a result, the bulk of typographic expertise and finesse is no longer available, and the quality of typography has deteriorated. (We'll discuss the art of typography in depth in Section 2.)

As time has gone by, we have seen little change in composition technology, except advances in speed and capability. Changes affecting the printing of documents are another issue entirely. Instead of printing to individual sheets of film, fully imposed flats are imaged. Even beyond that, direct-to-plate or direct-to-press imaging is common in many parts of the printing industry, allowing on-demand printing and variable-data printing.

Publishing Beyond Paper

No discussion of the evolution of publishing would be complete without considering the effects of documents that will never be printed in the traditional sense — they are designed to exist as electronic documents. Those documents appear as Web pages and multimedia documents; some exist as e-books, designed to read on the computer screen.

As early as the 1960s, the Internet began to take shape as the U.S. Department of Defense began investigating means of linking a number of computer installations so they could communicate even in the event of a nuclear war. Through its Advanced Research Projects Agency, the DOD initiated ARPANet, linking a number of military and university computers. In these early stages, operating protocols were established that allowed relatively fast and error-free transmission of data from computer to computer.

As ARPANet grew through the 1970s, other networks came into existence, including UUCP (Unix to Unix Copy) and USENET (the Users' Network). In 1981, with just over 200 computers connected to ARPANet, the military divided it into two organizations, ARPANet and a purely military network. ARPANet was absorbed by the National Science Foundation's NSFNET in the 1980. Eventually, the collection of networks became known as the "Internet."

The Internet grew slowly during these early years because users had to master complex sets of programming commands that required memorization or reference to special manuals. In 1991, British computer scientist Tim Berners-Lee developed what became known as the World Wide Web, using HyperText Markup Language (HTML) to link information.

In 1993, browsers were developed, and this further simplified the use of the Internet. In addition, tools that allowed point-and-click development of Web pages, coupled with more powerful computers, have brought about the tremendous growth of the Internet. Compare the 200 computers connected to ARPANet in 1981 to the tens of millions of users who access the Internet daily in 2001, with the anticipation of exponential growth.

With the growth of the Internet came the spread of shareware and freely distributed files, including fonts. Some of these are very well done and others are not, lacking sophisticated hinting and kerning pairs. In general, we recommend using only fonts from experienced professional and reputable foundries.

Fonts Used for Publishing

Although there are other font formats in limited use, Adobe Systems' Type 1 PostScript format and TrueType, developed by Apple Computer and Microsoft, are the leading formats for type. OpenType, jointly supported by Adobe and Microsoft, allows both TrueType and Type 1 fonts to work together seamlessly.

PostScript fonts (the left two icons) are comprised of a screen font and a printer font. TrueType fonts (with three "A"s) have the screen and printer data combined into one unit. OpenType fonts (right) are a super set of TrueType fonts that give the ability to access a broad range of glyphs.

The fonts using these technologies are unique, in that they work with any PostScript imaging device. All characters and symbols are stored as outlines, so they may be condensed, expanded, elongated and skewed. Their basic shapes may be altered using special programs. They may even be disassembled and retained as artwork, using standard illustration programs.

No matter where the fonts are stored, they must eventually be sent to the printer. As a practical matter, fonts are stored in three different locations:

- **ROM-based** fonts are stored in the printer's read-only memory. They cannot be erased.

- **Printer disk-based** fonts are stored on the printer's hard drive or on a drive attached to the printer.

- **Downloadable** fonts are stored in the computer and are automatically sent to the printer as needed. These fonts are replaced as new fonts are sent to the printer.

The fonts must also be stored where the computer can reference them. On Windows-based computers, TrueType fonts and PostScript screen fonts are stored in the Windows\Fonts folder; PostScript printer fonts are stored in the PS Fonts folder. On the Macintosh, fonts are stored in the Fonts folder within the System folder.

Font-management programs come and go. Master Juggler and FontMinder are gone; new programs such as Diamondsoft's Font Reserve are becoming available. Adobe has announced that they have no plans to support Macintosh OSX with Adobe Type Manager.

As font libraries grew, it became awkward to have hundreds of fonts available at all times. Font-management programs such as Master Juggler and Suitcase on the Macintosh and Ares FontMinder for Windows were used to turn fonts "on" and "off." More recently, ATM Deluxe (Adobe Type Manager) is also used for font management on both platforms. When a font manager is used, the fonts may be stored in any location on the computer.

PostScript, TrueType and Open Type fonts also use a hinting technology that allows them to be used in either high-resolution or low-resolution devices. Because low-resolution devices have a much coarser grid, letterforms are often distorted. *Hinting* is a set of mathematical instructions added to a font to tell the imaging device how to distort the font at given sizes in order to best preserve the actual shape of the letterform. This subject is discussed in considerable depth in Chapter 8: *The Mechanics of Type*. The evolution of type styles will be discussed in Chapter 3.

Summary

The development of written forms of expression includes a number of disciplines, from the origins of language itself to the bits and bytes of computer technology. As we have become more complex as a people, our means of communication have improved, and, rather than becoming more elitist, as might be expected, they have reached out to embrace a wider group. We saw this with the evolution of the alphabet, the development of the printing press and the democratization of typesetting through the introduction of off-the-shelf hardware and software.

Endnote

Not surprisingly, the early DTP programs ran on the PC (before Windows) and under different languages than PostScript (since they were released before either the Macintosh or the PostScript language). Some of these products ran on a microcomputer, but were really high-end typesetting software, using phototypesetters as their output device, instead of laser or other personal printers.

Several products "almost made it to market," and of those that did, most failed the acid test of producing quality commensurate with their price tags. Some were caught up in buyouts and mergers. Few of the early programs are still in existence.

After PostScript, the primary programs released were:

FrameMaker, Frame Corporation — *used for technical documents. Later acquired by Adobe Systems*
PageMaker, Aldus Corporation — *PC (with run-time Windows), Macintosh. Later acquired by Adobe Systems*
QuarkXPress, Quark, Inc. — *Macintosh, later also Windows*
Ventura Publisher, Xerox Corporation — *PC under GEM, later under Windows. Now owned by Corel*
InDesign, Adobe Systems — *Macintosh, Windows*

While there are a number of low-end programs in today's market and a few high-end programs, those that have been successful in keeping market share in the professional publishing arena are PageMaker, FrameMaker and QuarkXPress. InDesign, introduced by Adobe in 2000 shows promise. All professional publishing programs use the PostScript language today.

CHAPTER 2

Type Basics

While it's good to know about the origins of type and get some general information about its evolution from a technical standpoint, most of us love type as art. We appreciate the letterform and the way that letters work together, either to form blocks of text or to create logotypes.

Documents are comprised of two primary elements: text and graphics. Of these, in most documents, there is vastly more text. Type and particularly typography, though, is more than the process of placing text into a document. Rather, the beauty of the type itself, when properly produced, is an integral part of the document's design. It is still appropriate, however, that type should be essentially invisible as an entity — it should carry the message without calling attention to itself.

Achieving invisibility is an art. Elements of a document may draw your attention because they are well done or badly done. Type that is poorly kerned, that is improperly justified or that uses improper punctuation characters screams as loudly as a display face used for body text, bold text or type reversed out of a background.

Today, people who work with word-processing and desktop-publishing programs have a wealth of typefaces from which to choose, but this has not always been the case. In the early 1980s, the laser printer brought real typefaces to the office and home environment. Prior to this period, we churned out documents using some form of impact printer — a typewriter or dot-matrix printer. While typewriters had fonts of a sort, and some even provided variable spacing, they had little or no control over character spacing. When we needed to typeset a document, such as a brochure, newsletter or ad, we obtained the services of a typesetting firm or a printer to do it for us.

Wide and narrow characters
Wide and narrow characters

Monospaced type, such as Courier (top line), has characters of identical widths, creating unsightly loose or tight areas in the type. Variable spaced letterforms, such as Clarendon (bottom line), interact to create text that reads easily.

Analyzing Letterforms

When they look at type, many people see little or no difference between one typeface and another. Yet it is the nuance of design that contributes to a typeface's character. In typographic terms, letters are called "glyphs." All the glyphs in a given typeface are that typeface's *character set*; collectively, they are also called a "font."

A glyph is any symbol used in written communication. It may be a letter, a punctuation mark or any other symbol.

Glyphs are comprised of specific elements. They may take different forms, and not all elements are a part of all letterforms; for example, serifs are absent from sans-serif typefaces. In this section, we will examine the elements designers build into letters, both visible and invisible.

Glyph Anatomy

Strokes are the primary structural component of glyphs, by which we recognize letters. Strokes may be horizontal, vertical, diagonal or curved. Let's dissect some letters and see what elements comprise them.

- **Stress.** Stress is the angle of a curved stroke, which suggests the stroke of a pen as if the letter were created by a pen that makes thick and thin strokes, like a scribe's pen. The stress of a letter defines its "feel."

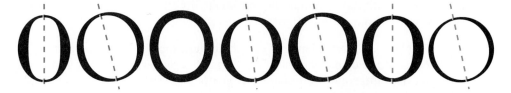

The letter "O" illustrates the stress of a letter well. Here, left to right, are the typefaces Bodoni Book, Goudy Oldstyle, Helvetica 55, Minion Regular, Palatino Regular, Times Roman and University Roman. Note that the sans-serif typeface, Helvetica, has no stress, but uses a uniform stroke.

- **Baseline.** The baseline is the imaginary line on which the "base" of letters sits. Descending letters, such as the g, j and y, extend below the baseline. In most typeface designs, rounded and pointed letters dip just below the baseline, giving them the appearance of sitting on it.

- **Stem.** The stem of a letter is the primary vertical stroke of a character, and does not include decorations, such as serifs or stroke endings. The vertical stroke in a T, b, l, p or h is a stem. In a character such as an H or an M, there are often primary and secondary stems.

- **Crossbar.** A horizontal stroke that crosses another stroke is a crossbar. They are found in the letters T, t and f.

- **Descender.** The descender extends below the baseline. Although we often refer to a "descender line," descenders within the same typeface may actually be of different depths. Descenders are found in the letters g, j, p, q and y.

- **Apex.** This is the point at the top of a letter where two strokes meet. They are found in the letters A, M, N, W and w.

- **Vertex.** This is the point where two strokes meet near the baseline of a letter. (The stroke may actually extend slightly below the baseline.) They are found in the letters M, V, W, v and w.

- **Ascender.** The part of a lowercase letter that extends above the x-height is called the "ascender." Ascenders are found in the letters b, d, f, h, k, l and t. In many lettering styles, the ascender is taller than the capital letter.

- **Spine.** This is the primary curve in the letter S.

- **Bar.** A bar is a horizontal stroke linking two strokes. Bars are found in the letters A, H and e.

- **Link.** The stroke tying together the upper and lower sections of the letter g, for example, is called the "link."

- **Loop.** The descender of a g, when it is entirely enclosed, is the loop. (When it is not enclosed, it is a tail.)

- **Ear.** The ear is a short protrusion on the letter g. Depending upon the typeface, it may also be found on the letters p and r.

- **Spur.** A spur is a short pointed projection from a stem or stroke, such as may be found on a C, G or t, depending on the design of the typeface.

- **Eye.** The enclosed space in the upper portion of the character e is called the "eye."

- **Terminal or Finial.** On a serif character, an ending other than a serif is called a "terminal" or a "finial." Terminals may be found in the letters C, c, e and t.

- **Counter.** A counter is an area entirely enclosed by a bowl or crossbar. Letters containing counters are B, O, P, Q, R, b, d, g, o, p and q.

- **Bowl.** A stroke surrounding a counter is called a "bowl."

- **Tail.** A tail is an extension projecting downward from a letter and usually falling below the baseline. It is attached at one end and unattached at the other, as on a Q or j. Some also call legs tails.

- **Arm.** An arm is a horizontal or upward diagonal stroke, attached to the letter at one end and unattached at the other. Arms are found on the letters K, V, W, X, Y, k, v, w, x and y.

- **Leg.** A downward diagonal stroke, attached to the letter at one end and unattached at the other is called a "leg." Legs are found on the letters K, R, X, k and x.

- **Swash.** A swash is a flourished terminal, stem or stroke added to a character. Swashes may be added at virtually any point in a letter.

- **Serif.** A serif is a beginning or finishing line drawn at a right angle or an oblique angle to the stem or stroke. The word comes from the Dutch word, *shreef*, which means line.

- **Shoulder.** A rounded portion of a lowercase letter that connects two vertical stems or strokes is called the "shoulder." Letters having shoulders are the e, h m and n.

- **Bracket or Fillet.** A curved or sloping shape that joins the serif to the stem or stroke is called a "bracket" or "fillet."

- **Kerning.** Kerning is an interaction between two letters that overlaps bounding boxes or pushes them apart. For example, in a To combination, the bounding boxes overlap in order to do away with the large "hole" that would develop under the crossbar of the T.

> *Kerning, a design element, is completely invisible, but very important for determining how easy a font will be to use. Well-designed type has many kerning pairs built into the typeface.*

Measuring Type

When deciding what typeface to use in a document, it is important to know what size type you will use and how much space that type will consume. Type size is measured vertically. Its horizontal measurement is defined as the number of characters per pica, inch or millimeter, assuming a normal combination of letters.

There are three systems for measuring type: the American/British point system, developed by Nelson C. Hawks in the 1870s; the Didot point system, developed by P.S. Fournier and F.A. Didot in the 18th century; and the metric system, used in much of Europe. The point system is used in the United States.

In the point system, there are 12 points to a pica. Each point is equal to 0.01383 inches, so each pica equals 0.166 inches. A PostScript point, in general use today, assigns an even 72 points (6 picas) to an inch, simplifying the measurement system.

Using the Didot point system, there are 12 Didot points to a Cicero. Each point is equal to 0.1483 inches, with a Cicero equaling 0.178 inches. As you note, Didot points are somewhat larger than American/British points.

The millimeter system uses the standard units of measure, millimeters, centimeters and meters to measure elements. There are approximately 2.85 American/British points in a millimeter.

Throughout this publication, we will use the American/British point system.

When measuring a typeface vertically, the overall height is measured from the bottom of the descender to the body clearance line — the space built in above the letters so type can be set with no additional line spacing (leading). Since this space is invisible and varies from one typeface to another, you can never accurately tell the type size by measuring the physical letters.

All type sits on a baseline. The height of a capital letter is called the "cap height." Letters with ascenders frequently extend above the cap height, and when this is the case, the font has a separate ascender height. The x-height is considered the height of lowercase letters, although rounded letters often shoulder above the x-height. Figures (numbers) may also have their own figure height. Small caps usually are slightly taller than the x-height.

Each type family has its own relative heights. Notice in this example (Minion), how much space the body clearance line allows above the letters. Rounded letters shoulder above the x-height and dip below the baseline. The proportion of the x-height to the cap height is an element that has a major impact on the legibility of a typeface.

The standard for horizontal measurement of type is the em. An *em* is a measurement equal in width to the point size specified. An em in 10-point type is 10 points wide; an em in 18-point type is 18 points wide. Often the em is described as a square the width and height of the point size specified.

☐ em in 10 pt. type

☐ em in 18 pt. type

The em is a fixed space equal to the specified point size.

If you are not given the character count (number of characters per pica), you will have to derive it in order to predetermine the size type you can use to fill a given area. This is not difficult. Simply take the width of the lowercase alphabet in points and divide 342 by that number.

0	24	48	72	96	120	144	168		
abcdefghijklmnopqrstuvwxyz								6 pt. Times Roman	78 pts.
abcdefghijklmnopqrstuvwxyz								6 pt. Stone Sans	84 pts.
abcdefghijklmnopqrstuvwxyz								8 pt. Times Roman	103 pts.
abcdefghijklmnopqrstuvwxyz								8 pt. Stone Sans	112 pts.
abcdefghijklmnopqrstuvwxyz								10 pt. Times Roman	129 pts.
abcdefghijklmnopqrstuvwxyz								10 pt. Stone Sans	140 pts.
abcdefghijklmnopqrstuvwxyz								12 pt. Times Roman	154 pts.
abcdefghijklmnopqrstuvwxyz								12 pt. Stone Sans	168 pts.

The 12-pt. Stone Sans alphabet is 168 pt. wide. We used the formula 342/168 and derived a character count of 2.04 characters per pica. Using the formula, determine how many characters per pica you have when using 10-pt. Times Roman.

After you know how many characters per pica (cpp) you have, you can approach copy fitting in one of two ways. You can determine how many characters you have (your word processor will give you a character count); you then divide the character count by the number of characters per pica. (If you have a 750-character ad, and you are using 10-pt. Times Roman, use the formula 150/2.65 = 283 picas). Alternately, you can determine how much space you have in picas, and then multiply by the number of characters per pica to determine how much text you can use. (If you have 400 picas available, and you are using 10-pt. Stone Sans, use the formula $400 \times 2.04 = 816$ characters).

If you know the character count for one size, you can calculate the character count for any other size. Since you know that 10-pt. Times Roman is 2.65 ccp, you can use the formula $2.65/1.2$ to determine the characters per pica in 12-pt. type, or $2.65/0.9$ to determine the characters per pica in 9-pt. type.

> *Even though type size can be changed at the touch of a button, it is still a good thing to learn the principles of type specification, particularly if you are writing to fill a given space.*

Typically, the problem with which you will be presented is a little stickier. You will know how many characters you have and how much area you have available to fill; your job is to determine what size type to use. We usually set up a chart to help us visualize what we are doing.

Characters	Width	Depth	Leading	Total Lines	Total Picas	CPP
2500	30	360	10	36	1080	2.31
			11	33	990	2.52
			12	30	900	2.78
			13	28	840	2.98

Here we divide the total depth in points by the leading to obtain the total lines. The formula Width ¥ Total Lines gives us our Total Picas. Divide Characters by Total Picas to find the necessary CPP.

In the example above, we determine the type size and leading as follows.

- Width × Total Lines = Total Picas: In 11 pt type, this is $30 \times 33 = 990$

- Characters ÷ Total Picas = Maximum CPP: $2500 \div 990 = 2.52$

- Select a type size with approximately 2.52 characters per pica and set it with 11 points of leading.

Specifying type using this method was absolutely necessary when type was ordered from an outside vendor. Even though type size can now be changed at the touch of a button, it is still useful to learn the principles, particularly if you are writing to fill a given space.

Font Basics

Often people speak about "fonts," using the term interchangeably with "type." While this is often acceptable in general conversation, it isn't technically correct.

A *font*, traditionally, is a specific typeface in a single point size. Because PostScript and TrueType fonts are scaled on the fly from a single printer font, today's font no longer has the single-point-size limitation. Standard fonts include the 26 uppercase and lowercase letters and numbers, plus additional characters such as punctuation, accents, international language characters, daggers, paragraph marks, symbols and more.

Specialized character sets — symbol (pi) and ornamental fonts — are an exception, often having no letters at all. There is even a font in the Poetica collection that is made up exclusively of ampersands.

Not all fonts contain the same letters — especially in the extended character set. Weight variations of the same font (bold, italic, light, etc.), however, usually contain the same characters. Even fonts with the same name but from different font foundries may have different character sets. Display fonts, designed to be used only in larger sizes, may lack characters found in text fonts. For example, Stencil Black has only uppercase characters, as do many "grunge" or "garage" fonts. "Expert" character sets contain supplemental characters, but not the standard characters of a font.

Even though the font is the same, at first glance, the extended characters for University Roman are different in the Adobe and the Font Company version.

What makes this complexity even more frustrating is that Windows and Macintosh systems do not have the same character sets, either. Twenty-three Macintosh characters are not duplicated in a Windows font set. Seventeen Windows characters are not duplicated in a Macintosh font set. To make matters worse, Windows and Macintosh code to select specific type characters is different (entering the same code number will access a different character). This is called the "encoding vector." Each font you buy from a major vendor contains both Windows and Macintosh character sets, but the encoding vector determines which characters will be used.

ÁÀÂÄÃÅáàâäãåÇçÉÈÊËéèêë
ÍÌÎÏíìîïÓÒÔÖÕóòôöõÚÙÛÜ
úùûüÑñŠšÝýŸÿðÞþ†°¢£§¶•ß
®©™´¨≠Æ×Ø∞±¹²³≤≥¥µ∂∑
∏π∫ªºΩæø¼½¾¿¡¬√ƒ≈∆«»‹›
…Œœ – —""'''÷◊/¤fifl‡·‰Ð

🍎₁ ^~ ˘˙˚ ˝ ˇ
, ˛

In the illustration above, the blue letters are found only on Windows systems, and the gray letters are available only on Macintosh systems.

From a practical standpoint, what does this mean?

If we use the upper level of characters (those with ASCII or ANSI codes above 128), it is a good idea to advise anyone printing the file, such as a GASP (Graphic Arts Service Provider), on what platform the document was created. Otherwise, we might type a bullet on a Windows system (ANSI character 149) and have ellipses result (ASCII character 149 on a Macintosh).

ASCII is the American Standard Code for Information Interchange. ANSI is the American National Standards Institute, the United States member of ISO, the International Standards Organization.

However, recent versions of most major word-processing and publishing programs have built-in cross-platform translation. If a document is created in Word on the Macintosh and opened in Word for Windows the ASCII characters will translate correctly — provided characters unique to the Macintosh were not used.

Occasionally, an entire font will be substituted. If the font is not resident, the printer's default font — usually Courier — will be substituted. In the virtual world, if the computer viewing a document does not have the appropriate font, the default font will be substituted, as well.

Dos and Don'ts

When publishing using microcomputers (dubbed "desktop publishing") emerged in the mid 1980s, the laser printer was new — and it shipped with 35 fonts: the ITC Avant Garde, ITC Bookman, Courier, Helvetica, Helvetica Narrow, New Century Schoolbook, Palatino and Times families of Regular, Italic, Bold and Bold Italic, plus Zapf Chancery and pi fonts Symbol and Zapf Dingbats. People just getting a taste of working with a selection of type didn't take the time to learn to use type well, or to learn customs that evolved over centuries. As a result, they often tried to use all 35 fonts in a single document, creating typographic nightmares.

Avant Garde *Oblique* **Demi** *Demi Oblique*
Bookman *Italic* **Demi** *Demi Italic*
Courier *Oblique* **Bold** *Bold Oblique*
Helvetica *Oblique* **Bold** *Bold Oblique*
Helvetica Narrow *Oblique* **Bold** *Bold Oblique*
NC Schoolbook *Italic* **Bold** *Bold Italic*
Palatino *Italic* **Bold** *Bold Italic*
Times Roman *Italic* **Bold** *Bold Italic*
Zapf Chancery
Symbol ΑΒΧΔΕΦΓαβχδεφγ ≡ ∂↔⊗♥∫⌊↔⌈⌡
Zapf Dingbats ✪✛✢✣✤✥✦✧❀❂❉✳✴✵✶✷❁⑤❩☜

These "standard 35" fonts shipped with most laser printers in the mid 1980s. It really was not necessary to use every font in every document, although many tried.

Typographic abuses still abound, many of them based on the standards set for old monospaced typing. Later in this book, we'll delve into a variety of ways to work with spacing and other elements. For now, however, let's look at some *Dos and Don'ts* that are basic to typography, and may run counter to what is taught in standard word-processing courses.

- Do put a single space after periods, colons and similar punctuation.

- Do use hyphens, en dashes and em dashes correctly. Don't use two hyphens instead of a dash.

- Don't insert a tab or spaces at the beginning of a paragraph. Your program will automatically insert any indent.

- Do insert one tab for every tabular field. Don't try to align tabular copy using multiple tabs.

- Don't add periods for leader dots. The program will insert appropriate leader characters when the tab is programmed to do so.

- Do use true quotation marks and apostrophes. Don't use the prime and double prime found on the keyboard.

- Don't forget that not all translation is automatic. You need to insert the apostrophe manually before abbreviations of years, such as '01.

- Do use inch, foot and multiplication symbols (from the symbol font). Don't use the double prime, prime or x.

- Do place all periods, commas and punctuation "belonging to the quotation" within quotation marks, unless you are writing for the UK market.

- Do use a smaller point size for acronyms and other uppercase text.

- Do add letterspace when using all caps and small caps. Don't add letterspace to lowercase letters.

- Do use a slightly smaller size for numbers, unless you are using oldstyle numbers.

- Do use the ellipsis character (…). Don't use three spaced (or unspaced) periods.

- Do use the discretionary hyphen. Don't expect the program to hyphenate appropriately.

- Do adjust the size and position of ballot boxes and bullets so they match the typeface you are using.

- Do use your spell-checker. Don't neglect to proofread the document with your own eyes. (Both *worn* and *worm* are words, but there's a huge difference in meaning.)

- Do type in sentence case. Don't type in all caps. If you think you'll need capitals, use the capitalization tool from the menu. Most DTP programs can't uncapitalize if you need to change back, and you'll have to retype all the text.

- Do use boldface sparingly. Don't use underlines, shadowed letters or outlined letters from the selection menu.

- Don't use the palette's Bold or Italic in place of selecting the actual font (for example, Minion Bold) unless you are sure of what the font call will be. For example, clicking on Bold to style Minion will access Minion Semibold, not Minion Bold.

Summary

In this chapter, you have learned to analyze glyphs to identify the parts of letters. You have also learned how to specify type mathematically, so you are not entirely dependent upon the computer when you embark on a project — you'll have a starting place. In addition, you have learned some differences between character sets on Windows and on Macintosh-based computers.

Finally, you have learned some basic typographic dos and don'ts. Applying them will not only help you create better documents, it will save you untold embarrassment and costly mistakes.

As we move through our discussion of type and typography, you will discover that type is far more than a collection of alphabets — it is both an artistic expression of the designer and a highly technical assemblage of detail. Typography affects our comprehension of text, and it affects the overall design of the document.

As the book progresses, you will explore typography as science, experience the art of typography and work with combining type in various ways with rules and graphics. You will discover how type can be used as an element of design, or as the entire designed element. You will explore the uses of type on the Internet, and become aware of the pitfalls that await. Finally, you will delve into the mechanics of type and learn to manage fonts for display and for printing.

CHAPTER 3

Exploring Categories of Type

Creating attractive documents using type doesn't happen automatically. Selecting the right type for the job is an art, as is effectively and efficiently controlling the type on the page — whether it is to be printed or will remain in electronic form.

In this chapter, we will examine the primary categories of type, looking at some of the fonts within the larger categories. We will observe basic character sets and explore reasons for using each, in preference to settling for only basic sets.

In Chapter 2, you learned that glyphs are part of a character set, or font, and that fonts, in turn, are often grouped into families. In this chapter, you will explore a number of type categories and learn about some of the systems devised for grouping type families.

Categorizing Type

It is important to have a basis from which to discuss the appearance of different type styles. To this end, a number of systems have been devised, each with its own strengths and weaknesses, and each with its own goals. Because of these differing goals, they often use conflicting definitions of typographic terms, such as the word "Roman." In one classification system this term means the typeface that has elegant, sloping serifs, and a clear distinction between thick and thin strokes. In others it means the base (non-italic, non-bold) face of a family of type, which is how the term is used in this book.

In still others it is used in place of the word "serif." The type classification systems are:

- **The De Vinne System.** This system, devised by Theodore Low De Vinne, New York, 1900, uses nine primary categories, and a number of subcategories. His categories are: Roman Form of Type, Modernized Old-Style, Modern Faces of Roman Letter, Italic, Fat Face or Title, Black-Letter, Gothic, Antique, Old-Style and Doric Antiques.

- **The Vox System.** This system, devised by Maximillan Vox, France, 1954, also uses nine primary categories. His categories are: Humanes (derived from hand lettering), Garaldes (French 16th-century styles), Réales (18th-century styles), Didones (late 18th-century styles), Incises (modeled after 1st- and 2nd-century letterform), Linéales (Sans Serif faces), Mécanes (square-serif typestyles), Scriptes and Manuaires (20th-century styles designed on a pantograph machine).

- **The Novarese System.** This system, by Aldo Novarese, Italy, 1956, uses 10 primary categories. His classifications are: Veneziani (15th-century Venetian), Elziviri (Renaissance), Transizionali (faces inspired by the Romain de Roi), Bodoniani (faces with strong vertical stress), Egizani (Egyptian and Slab Serif), Lineari (Sans Serif), Lapidari (type with a chiseled effect), Scritti (Script), Fantasie (Art Nouveau and other "fancy" type) and Medieval (Blackletter).

- **The AtypI System.** This system, by the Association Typographique Internationale, Paris, 1961 uses 10 categories. Their categories are: Humane (15th-century romans), Garalde (16th-century French), Réale (Transitional), Didone (Modern), Mécane (Square Serif), Linéale (Sans Serif), Incise (type with wedge-shaped serifs), Scripte, Manuaire (Display) and Fractura (Blackletter).

- **The DIN Schriften System.** This system, devised by Hermann Zapf, 1967 uses three primary categories with a number of subcategories. His categories are: Roman (with subcategories Renaissance, Baroque, Neo-classic, Free Roman [which includes sans-serif], Linear, Block Roman, Script), Blackletter and Non-roman characters.

- **The Typefinder System.** This system, devised by Christopher Perfect and Gordon Rookledge in 1983, uses 2 primary and 16 secondary categories. This system was devised to help people to identify typefaces easily. Text typefaces are: Sloping e-bar (Venetian Serif), Angled Stress/Oblique Serifs (Old Style Serif), Vertical Stress/Oblique Serifs (Transitional Serif), Vertical Stress/Straight Serifs (New Transitional Serif), Abrupt Contrast/Straight Serifs (Modern Serif), Slab Serif, Wedge Serif (Hybrid Serif) and Sans Serif. Decorative (noncontinuous text) typefaces are: Flowing Scripts, Non-flowing Scripts (including Blackletter and Uncial), Unmodified (Formal Text Shape), Fat & Thin Face (modified and unmodified), Ornamental, Modified Serif, Modified Sans Serif and Modified Outrageous.

- **The Lawson System.** This system, by Alexander S. Lawson, 1971, uses a more nearly historic basis for its classification into eight broad categories. We use the Lawson System in the following section, "Evolution of Type Styles." His categories are: Blackletter, Old-style, Transitional, Modern, Square Serif, Sans Serif, Script/Cursive/Brush and Decorative/Display.

Evolution of Type Styles

As we discussed in Chapter 1, written language evolved over thousands of years. Type-setting, though, is just over half a millennium in age, dating from 1448 and Gutenberg's development of movable type. In this section, we'll examine how different styles of type came into being, and how we can identify type within their categories. There are several methods of classification of type styles. We will group them into nine primary categories, and then include subcategories when appropriate. The nine categories are: Blackletter, Oldstyle, Transitional, Modern, Slab Serif, Sans Serif, Script (including nonflowing scripts), Decorative/Display and Pi. We have added a Pi category because these typefaces do not fit comfortably within the Lawson system, and they are too important to be ignored.

Blackletter

The first type styles closely imitated the brush and pen strokes made by the scribes. At the earlier stages of publishing, part of the goal of the compositor/printer was to make the document look as similar as possible to expensive handcrafted work. These type-faces include heavy Germanic-looking faces, elegant Olde English and a variety of Uncial hands. Here are some representative samples.

Poetica Chancery

Poetica Chancery, designed in 1993 by Robert Slimbach, is representative of the chancery style used by scribes pre-Gutenberg. The font family has some delightful swash capitals and a variety of alternate characters. There is even a "font" consisting of ampersands. Chanceries, while included here for historical purposes, are also included in the Scripts classification.

Wittenberger Fraktur
Wilhelm Klingspor Gotisch
Fette Fraktur

Letterforms such as these predominated in the Germanic countries, and were carried into the printed word. Type similar to these faces was used for text in Germany until World War II. The Monotype Design Staff designed Wittenberger Fraktur in 1903, Rudolph Koch designed Wilhelm Klingspor Gotisch in 1925, and C.E. Weber designed Fette Fraktur in 1875.

Clairvaux
Duc De Berry
San Marco

Fonts such as these have a Renaissance feel to them, and generally are regarded to be in the Blackletter category. Clairvaux was designed by Herbert Maring in 1981, Duc De Berry was designed by Gottfried Pott in 1990, and San Marco was designed by Karlgorg Hoefer in 1990. All are part of the Linotype's Type Before Gutenberg 2 collection.

Olde English
Goudy Text
Goudy Text/Lombardic

The Olde English look is shared by Engravers Olde English (Morris Fuller Benton, 1901) and Goudy Text (Frederic W. Goudy, 1927–29). The Lombardic capitals give the Goudy Text style a unique flair.

Although not technically Blackletter fonts, illuminates such as these were used extensively in continental Europe and in the British Isles. These letters are taken from the Book of Kells, and represent the letters A, H, M and U. The Book of Kells is an Irish manuscript containing the four Gospels, a fragment of Hebrew names and the Eusebian canons. It dates from the late-7th or early-8th century.

Oldstyle

The Oldstyle category of type began with the first roman face, designed by Nicholas Jensen in 1470 and with the first italic, designed by Aldus Manutius in 1471. Both these letter types were designed in Venice, hence our Italian names for roman and italic fonts.

Designers Claude Garamond, Robert Granjon and Jean Jannon in the 16th century were influenced by Oldstyle form. The style carried into the early years of the 18th century, when it also influenced Christoffel Van Dijck in Holland and William Caslon in England. Many modern faces copy the style of these early masters.

Aldus Corporation, creators of PageMaker, one of the first successful desktop-publishing programs, honored Aldus Manutius by naming their company after him. Adobe Systems purchased Aldus in 1994.

Characteristics

The Oldstyle typefaces have a consistent stroke weight and the stress is slightly inclined to the left. Early Oldstyle typefaces exhibit a diagonal crossbar on the lowercase "e" and an ascender height similar to that of capital letters; in later Oldstyles, this stroke is usually horizontal and the ascenders are taller than the capitals.

Where appropriate and available, we show examples of small capitals, oldstyle figures and swash characters.

Aldus *Aldus*
ALDUS 1234 *1234*

This typeface, adopted by Aldus Corporation (later purchased by Adobe Systems), is representative of the works of Nicholas Jensen and Aldus Manutius. Hermann Zapf designed Aldus in 1954. The typeface has one weight, plus small caps and oldstyle figures.

Adobe Garamond
Adobe Garamond
ADOBE GARAMOND 1234

Adobe Garamond, designed by Robert Slimbach in 1989, is representative of the typeface designed by Claude Garamond around 1530. Adobe Garamond has four weights and an expert character set.

Claude Garamond, born in Paris in 1490, was the first independent type founder. Garamond was the first to make type available to printers at an affordable price.

Granjon *Granjon*
GRANJON 1234 *1234*

Granjon, designed by George W. Jones in 1958, is similar to typefaces designed by Robert Granjon in the early 1500s. Granjon has two weights and an expert character set.

Van Dijck *Van Dijck*
OLDSTYLE 1234 *1234*

Van Dijck, designed by the Monotype Design Staff and Jan Van Krimpen in 1937, closely resembles the work of Christoffel van Dyck around 1660. Van Dijck has a single weight.

Adobe Caslon *Caslon*
CASLON 1234 *1234*

Carol Twombly designed Adobe Caslon in 1990. As is true with so many of the Adobe Originals series, it carries the feel of the original designer's work. William Caslon designed a similar typeface in 1725. This version includes three weights, expert sets and swash characters.

Born in 1692, William Caslon set up his type foundry in London in 1716. Among the famous documents set in one of his type-faces was the first printing of the American Declaration of Independence.

Minion *Minion*
MINON 1234 *1234*

Minion, designed by Robert Slimbach in 1989 as part of the Adobe Originals series, carries the feel of the Oldstyle category of type. Minion includes five weights, expert sets, swash characters and ornaments.

Transitional

This stage of type development was begun near the end of the 17th century. A committee under the auspices of the French Acadêmie des Science was formed to create a new and improved type style for use by the royal printing office. They created a font known as "Romain du Roi," which included a greater difference between thick and thin strokes and serifs that were sharp and straight. Almost simultaneously, Hungarian designer Nikolas Kis was creating type with similar characteristics. Fifty years later, Pierre Simon Fournier introduced type with similar features, and in 1757 John Baskerville introduced a comparable font of his own design. These fonts are transitional between fonts having the relatively consistent stroke weight with strongly bracketed serifs and those having contrasting stroke weights with unbracketed serifs (the Modern category).

Characteristics

Transitional type features greater contrast between stroke weights and sharp, straight serifs. The stress of curved strokes is nearly vertical.

New Caledonia
New Caledonia

New Caledonia, designed in 1978 by John Quaranta, is an adaptation of William Addison Dwiggins's 1938 typeface, Caledonia. Caledonia is a popular typeface for book publishing. New Caledonia has four weights.

Fairfield *Fairfield*
FAIRFIELD 1234 *1234*

In 1991, Alex Kakzun adapted Rudolph Ruzikas's 1938 design for Fairfield. This type family has four weights, small caps, and swash and oldstyle figures. Note the use of ligatures to bring the fi character combination together.

Bulmer *Bulmer*

In 1928, Morris Fuller Benton adapted British designer William Martin's 1790 design for Bulmer. The Bitstream version of this font (used here) has one weight. The Monotype version, designed by Ron Carpenter in 1994, has five weights plus expert font sets.

Times New Roman
Times New Roman

Times New Roman is representative of the font originally designed in 1932 for the Times of London by Stanley Morrison, Victor Lardent and the Monotype Design Staff. Times has become the standard serif typeface of the computer industry. Versions of this font are available in four weights, and some include expert sets.

Stone Serif
Stone Serif

Sumner Stone created ITC Stone Serif in 1987 in three weights. It is a completely contemporary font in the Transitional style.

Modern

The Modern category of type is often considered elegant, and is frequently used in magazine ads — especially for high fashion products. Because there are often extremes of contrast between thick and thin strokes, these typefaces work well for headlines and short body copy. They can be tiring to read in long passages of text. The designs began in the late-18th and early-19th centuries with the creations of Giambattista Bodoni and Firmin Didot. Later this style was employed by Justus Erich Walbaum and by a number of English and Scottish designers.

Characteristics

The most recognizable feature of Modern typefaces is the contrast between thick and thin strokes. In some cases, this ranges between an extremely heavy stroke and one of hairline width. The serifs are usually thin and flat, with little or no bracketing. The stress is vertical.

Bauer Bodoni
Bauer Bodoni
Bauer 1234 *1234*
Poster/*Italic*
Compressed

Giambattista Bodoni, who designed type in the late-18th and early-19th centuries, was one of the most productive type designers of all time. Notice particularly how the radical difference between thick and thin strokes is epitomized in the design of the Poster and Compressed faces. Heinrich Jost designed Bauer Bodoni in 1926, and Morris Fuller Benton designed Poster Bodoni in 1910.

> *Bodoni has been called the father of Modern type. His elegant books were made to be admired for type and layout; he was indifferent to content. His mechanical perfection in typography was considered by some to be the ultimate example of modern ugliness.*

Linotype Didot
Linotype Didot
Didot 1234 *1234*

Linotype Didot, designed by Adrian Frutiger in 1991, is similar to the typeface designed by Firmin Didot in 1784. The typeface is available in three weights, with small caps, oldstyle figures and ornaments.

Walbaum
Walbaum

Justus Erich Walbaum designed the original Walbaum typeface around 1803. Günter Gerhard Lange designed this version, Berthold Walbaum, which includes three weights, in 1975. A Monotype version was designed in 1934.

Linotype Centennial
Linotype Centennial
CENTENNIAL 1234 *1234*

Linotype Centennial is a contemporary Modern face, designed by Adrian Frutiger in 1986. There are four weights, small caps and oldstyle figures.

Scotch Roman
Scotch Roman

Designed by A.D. Farmer in 1904, this font is representative of those of Scottish and English designers. It is a redesign of the typeface by Robert Austin around 1813.

Melior *Melior*
Melior

Hermann Zapf designed Melior in 1952. Although the thick/thin difference is not pronounced in the roman weight, it becomes more obvious in the bold weight of this font.

Fenice *Fenice*
Fenice Fenice

Designed by Aldo Novarese in 1980, this font is very similar to Melior. While it has a higher x-height and is narrower, the feel of the letterform is very similar, including the absence of a true italic. (The "italic" is designed as an oblique for both fonts.) Fenice has four weights; shown here are regular, bold and ultra.

Slab Serif

The Slab Serif category of type is a clear evolution from the Modern typefaces, with less contrast between thick and thin strokes. The earliest designs were from English founder Vincent Figgins. These typefaces had a single weight — even to the unbracketed serifs — and were called "Antique." The first of these was available only in capital letters. Later, the Egyptian group of Slab Serif typefaces was developed, with a lower case and bracketed serifs. In the mid-19th century, typefaces with varying weights, called "Clarendons," were introduced. Many typewriter faces and newspaper faces are Slab Serifs.

Characteristics

Like the Modern style from which they came, the Slab Serif typefaces generally exhibit a vertical stress. While there is some variation in the stroke weight of many faces, it is very nearly consistent throughout each letterform. Serifs are very heavy — sometimes the same weight as the primary stroke of the character.

Stymie *Stymie*

Stymie was designed n 1931 by Morris Fuller Benton and epitomizes the earlier forms of the Slab Serif category. It has four weights, plus a condensed version.

Lubalin Graph
Lubalin Graph

ITC Lubalin Graph was designed by Herb Lubalin in 1974 — a serif version of the popular Avant Garde Gothic designed by Lubalin in cooperation with Tom Carnase. Like Avant Garde and Stymie, it has an oblique rather than a true italic. Lubalin Graph has five weights and four condensed weights.

Egyptienne
Egyptienne

This typeface, designed in 1953 by Adrian Frutiger, is representative of the Egyptian subcategories of the Slab Serif category. This typeface has two weights and a true italic.

Clarendon

Hermann Eidenbenz designed Clarendon in 1951, exemplifying the Clarendon subcategory of Slab Serifs. The font is unique in that it has no accompanying italic, but is available in five weights plus two condensed versions.

Cheltenham
Cheltenham

ITC Cheltenham, designed by Tony Stan in 1975, is the most recent version of the Cheltenham typeface. (Ed Benguiat designed a hand-tooled version based on this face in 1993.) It has four weights in the regular width and in its condensed version. Earlier versions of Cheltenham, with a much higher ascender and lower x-height were designed by Bertram C. Goodhue in 1896 and by Morris Fuller Benton in 1904.

Prestige Elite
Prestige Elite

Prestige Elite, designed by Clayton Smith in 1953 for use on typewriters, is a monospaced typeface. It's very hard to make it look good, accustomed as we are to variable-spaced characters today.

An extreme example of the Slab Serif category is Ponderosa, designed by Kim Baker, Barbara Lind and Joy Reddick in 1990. This typeface can also be placed in the Decorative or Display category.

Sans Serif

Typefaces without (sans) serifs appeared for the first time in a type specimen issued by William Caslon IV in 1816. In 1833, before consistency in spelling was important, the name "sans surryph" was applied to the form, becoming the Sans Serif that we are familiar with today. Sans Serif typefaces that have uniform strokes are often called "Grotesques" or "Gothics"; this style of Sans Serif type was popular in England and Germany throughout the 19th century and into the early 20th century, when it expanded worldwide. Subcategories of Sans Serif type include the Geometric, Neo-Grotesque and Humanist type styles. A number of Sans Serif fonts use numeric designations for their width and weight.

In 1950, Adrian Frutiger designed a numeric palette for the Univers font with 21 variations in weight, width and orientation (roman or italic). As the years progressed, other foundries added to the Univers family. The Helvetica Neu family of type uses the Frutiger numeric system. The first digit indicates the weight, with 1 being the lightest and 9 the heaviest. The second digit indicates the width, with 1 being theoretically the widest and 9 the narrowest. Roman faces use odd numbers, and italics or obliques use even numbers.

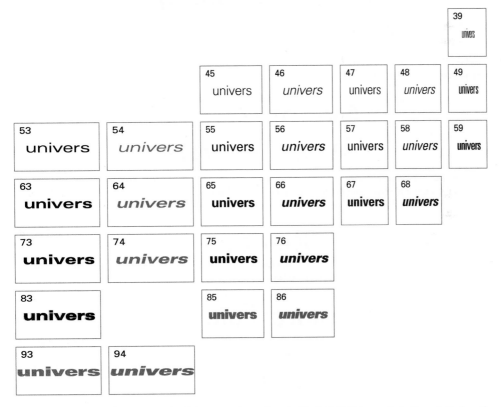

Frutiger's original 21 designations for Univers are shown here in black. Additions made to the palette by other foundries appear in color.

In the 1980s, David Berlow of The Font Bureau developed a somewhat different numbering system. The first digit indicates the width, with 1 as the narrowest and 9 as the widest. The second digit indicates the weight, with 1 as the lightest and 9 as the heaviest. As with the Frutiger system, roman faces use odd digits, while italic faces use even digits.

Sans-serif design was strongly influenced by the Bauhaus School (1919 – 33), founded by Walter Gropius in Weimer, Germany (and later moved to Dessau). The school taught that the worlds of fine art and the crafts — people building useful items — should be merged. Architecture, sculpture and painting should be unified as a single art form. After the National Socialist government in Germany dissolved the Bauhaus School, it was succeeded by the New Bauhaus in Chicago, Illinois. Many of the Bauhaus instructors immigrated to the United States to teach in the new school. Others taught in various universities across the U.S. Today, the New Bauhaus is known as the Institute of Design, part of the Illinois Institute of Technology.

Characteristics

The most striking feature of this category is the absence of serifs. Strokes tend to be similar in width, though the Neo-Grotesque and Humanist type styles display some contrast. The italics of many Sans Serif typefaces are, in fact, obliques rather than true italics, which experience a change in the shape of some letters.

Akzidenz Grotesque
Akzidenz Grotesque

Designed in 1900 by H. Berthold AG, Akzidenz Grotesque features consistent strokes throughout. There are five weights and condensed and expanded widths.

Avant Garde
Avant Garde

Herb Lubalin and Tom Carnase designed ITC Avant Garde Gothic in 1970. The family of type was expanded by André Gürtler, Christian Mengelt and Erich Geshwind in 1977. There are five weights in this family. In 1974, Ed Benguiat designed ITC Avant Garde Condensed in four weights.

Bauhaus

The Bauhaus School of Design influenced fonts in the Geometric subcategory. Ed Benguiat and Victor Caruso designed ITC Bauhaus in 1973 with five weights. It is based upon a design by Herbert Bayer from 1925.

Futura *Futura*

Futura, designed by Paul Renner in 1928, is probably the most popular of the Geometric type families. Futura has six weights. In 1930, Renner went on to design four weights of Futura Condensed.

Kabel

The ITC Design Staff created ITC Kabel in 1976, based on Rudolph Koch's 1927 design. This Geometric Sans Serif has five weights. Koch's original had four weights.

Helvetica Neu
Helvetica Neu

The Helvetica Neu family of type is one of the largest type families available, and is part of the Neo-Grotesque subcategory. It has eight weights plus an outline form, and includes both condensed and extended versions within the overall family. The Linotype Design Studio developed this family of type in 1983, based on earlier Helvetica designs by Max Miedinger and Edouard Hoffman in 1957.

Univers
Univers

Adrian Frutiger designed Univers in 1957. This Neo-Grotesque was the standard sans-serif font used on the IBM Selectric Composer. Univers has five standard weights, and also includes condensed, expanded and ultra-condensed families.

Gill Sans *Gill Sans*
SHADOWED
Light Shadowed

Eric Gill designed this early Humanist type family in 1928. It is available in seven weights plus three condensed weights. In addition, Gill Sans Display includes Shadowed (all uppercase) and Light Shadowed versions. The heaviest of the Gill fonts is called Gill Kayo.

Optima *Optima*

Hermann Zapf designed Optima, possibly the most recognizable of the Humanist typefaces, in 1958. Optima is available in six weights.

Frutiger *Frutiger*

Designed by Adrian Frutiger in 1976, this Humanist typeface has five weights, as does its condensed version.

Script, Cursive and Brush

While this category can be considered a spinoff of the Chancery models (as this classification system does), most people think of a Cursive or Script typeface as being similar to the first one cut by Robert Granjon in the mid-16th century. This was called "letter courant" in France and "secretary hand" in England. The category includes any connecting or nonconnecting style that appears to have been created with a pen or brush. These letters can be very delicate or very bold, formal or informal.

Characteristics

Regardless of the weight of the letters, or whether they appear to be informal or formal, all styles in this category appear to have been written or flowed onto the page, rather than being drawn. Technically, Chanceries are a part of this category, even though we have also included them in the Blackletter category for purposes of historic continuity.

$$Zapf\ Chancery$$
$$Zapf\ Chancery$$

Zapf Chancery, designed by Hermann Zapf in 1979, is one of the "standard 35" fonts that ship with all PostScript printers. The Zapf Chancery family has three weights, each with a roman and an italic.

$$Berthold\ Script$$
$$Vivaldi$$

Elegant Scripts, such as Berthold Script (two weights), designed by Günter Gernhard Lange in 1977, and Vivaldi, designed by Fritz Peters in 1970, are particularly useful for formal invitations.

$$Cataneo\ Isadora$$

Bitstream Cataneo, designed by Jacquelin Sakwa and Richard Lipton in 1993, is based on Bernardino Cataneo's 1545 version. There are three weights plus alternate and swash characters. ITC Isadora, designed by Kris Holmes in 1985, is a playful script with two weights.

$$Monoline\ Script$$
$$Caflisch\ Script$$

Monoline Script, designed by the Monotype Design Staff in 1933 and Caflisch Script, designed by Robert Slimbach as a Multiple Master font in 1993, are examples of attached scripts that have a single stroke weight.

> **Multiple Master, a subset of the Adobe Type 1 technology, will be discussed in Chapter 8.**

$$Kaufmann$$
$$Mistral$$

Kaufmann, designed by M.R. Kaufmann in 1936, and Mistral, designed by Roger Excoffon in 1953, are attached casual typefaces. Kaufmann has two weights while Mistral has one.

Comic Sans Sho

Casual, detached typefaces such as these appear to have been painted with a brush. Vincent Connare designed Comic Sans in 1995; it is part of Microsoft's Core Fonts for the Web collection. Karlgeorg Hoefer designed Sho in 1993.

Decorative/Display

Decorative or Display typefaces are meant to be used in headlines and to convey specific meaning — they are not to be used as text fonts. If we don't count the decorative woodcuts inserted into otherwise cast type, the earliest decorative typeface was likely Union Pearl, cut in England in 1690. Decorative typefaces were made available in England and France from the 18th century onward. They increased in numbers throughout the 19th and 20th centuries, largely in response to the demand of advertisers.

Characteristics

The only common characteristic of typefaces in this category is that they are intended to be used in larger sizes only. They vary widely in style and application.

ALGERIAN   Arnold Böcklin
BREMEN

Fonts such as these have flourishes added to the letters, making them suitable for display, but not for text. Phillip Kelley designed Algerian in 1988. Otto Weisert designed Arnold Böcklin for Linotype Corporation in 1904. Richard Lipton designed Bremen in 1992.

CaslonOpenface Mona Lisa
CASTELLAR SMARAG

Openface or engraved letters appear similar to letters chiseled into monuments. Caslon Openface was designed in 1915. John Peters designed Castellar in 1957. Pat Hickson redrew Mona Lisa in 1991 from Albert Auspurg's 1930 version. Gudrun Zapf-von Hesse designed Smarag in 1953.

Broadway Industria Inline

Fonts containing an inline stroke or an extra stroke, such as these, are fun to work with in headlines. If they are used at too small a size, the additional stroke blurs with the main strokes of the letter or simply disappears. Morris Fuller Benton designed Broadway Engraved and its companion font, Broadway, in 1927. Neville Brody designed Industria Inline and Industria Solid in 1990.

EMPIRE HUXLEY VERTICAL PLAZA

MACHINE STENCIL

MESQUITE PEPPERWOOD

Fonts that have no lower case provide interesting opportunities when creating headlines. As you see from these examples, they can create various images in your mind. Morris Fuller Benton designed Empire in 1937; David Berlow created a 1989 version containing lowercase letters. Walter Huxley designed Huxley Vertical in two weights in 1935; companion fonts are Huxley High and Huxley Low. Alan Meeks designed Plaza in 1975. Tom Carnase and Renne Bonder designed ITC Machine in 1970. Stencil is part of the Adobe Display Set #4 and was designed by Gerry Powell in 1938. Joy Redick designed Mesquite, part of Adobe Wood Type #1, in 1990. Kim Baker Chansler and Carl Crossgrove designed Pepperwood, part of Adobe Wood Type #3, in 1994.

Chwast Buffalo PTBarnum
Gorilla Hobo Revue

Some display faces use unique letterform to set them off. That is the case with these five typefaces. Seymour Chwast designed Chwast Buffalo Black Condensed in 1993. PT Barnum conveys the flavor of posters of a bygone age. ITC Gorilla, designed by Tom Carnase and Ronne Bonder in 1970, has heavy features and a "rough feel." Hobo, designed by Morris Fuller Benton in 1910, has a look of movement. Revue, designed by Colin Brignall in 1968, has an off-center sophistication, even though the glyphs are very heavy.

BernhardFashion

Onyx MisterEarl OzHandicraft

Ozwald

Even though these letterforms are normal, the x-height or character width makes them unacceptable for long-running text, but well suited for display and short advertising text. Lucian Bernhard designed Bernhard Fashion in 1929. Onyx is a 1937 creation of Gerry Powell. Jenny Maestre designed Mister Earl in 1991. Oz Handicraft is George Ryan's 1991 adaptation of Ozwald Cooper's rendition. ITC Ozwald is David Farey's 1992 update to Ozwald Cooper's 1928 design.

LITHOS

HERCULANUM

RUSTICANA

These three typefaces are reminiscent of early Greek and Roman writing forms, and give a specific feel to the page. Carol Twombly designed Lithos in 1989. Adrian Frutiger designed Herculanum and Rusticana in 1990 and 1993, respectively.

Quake
Visigoth Spumoni

Some fonts shake up your eyes, either by vibrating or by playing with the apparent baseline. Quake, designed by Fryda Berd in 1993 as part of the Adobe Wild Type collection, visibly vibrates. Visigoth, designed by Arthur Baker in 1988, combines its thick and thin strokes radically, often dropping letters below the baseline. Garrett Boge's 1988 design of Spumoni angles each letter, distorting our perspective of the baseline.

STOP UMBRA

Clear evidence that we "see" letters based on our experience, these typefaces are unique. They are perceived more by what is not there, than by what is. Stop, designed by Aldo Novarese in 1971, is part of Linotype's Headliners collection. Robert Hunter Middleton designed Umbra in 1932.

CRITTER MYTHOS

In a whimsical return to illustrated capital letters, these members of Adobe's Wild Type collection spark our interest. Craig Frazier designed Critter, and Jim Wasco and Min Wang designed Mythos. We picture them larger than other fonts in this series to better show their detail.

Pi

Pi characters, often called "symbol," "logo," "dingbat" or "ornaments," are used to insert symbols that are reused many times into text. These might include characters in a math font, a company logo, blocks in a crossword puzzle, borders for a page, credit cards, astrological symbols or map symbols. If there is a need, such a font is often created. This saves much time and space in documents, where a logo may even be used as a bullet point. There are hundreds of Pi fonts. We offer those below as a representative sampling.

Cleo Huggins designed Sonata in 1989. With a little work, you can actually write music using your computer.

myalgia / mīáljə / *n.* a pain in a muscle or group of muscles. myalgic *adj.* [mod. L. f. Gk *mus* muscle]

myalism / mīəlizəm / *n.* a kind of sorcery akin to obeah, practiced esp. in the W. Indies. [*myal*, prob. of W. Afr. orig.]

John Renner designed Stone Phonetic Sans and Stone Phonetic Serif in 1992, based on Sumner Stone's 1989 typeface design. All the characters are available to allow you to assign phonetic characters to IPA standards.

$$\sqrt{64} \times 3 = 24$$

Universal Greek with Math Pi is just one of many fonts that allow you to set type for higher math functions. This font, and its accompanying Universal News with Commercial Pi, comprise the Linotype Universal Pi collection.

Carta, designed by Lynne Garrell in 1986, contains many symbols used in mapmaking.

Agfa Credit Cards contains a number of credit card symbols that can easily be inserted on pages of a catalog.

Linotype Astrology Pi includes a number of varieties of astrological symbols, from simple line versions to more detailed illustrative versions of astrological signs.

Monotype Signs includes a number of symbols frequently used in signage and labeling.

Poetica Ornaments is an entire font of embellishments. Robert Slimbach designed them with the rest of the Poetica typeface in 1993.

| Control | Option | ⌘ | Alt | Delete | Return | Esc |

| A | B | C | D | ! 1 | @ 2 | # 3 | $ 4 |

Monotype Keystrokes allows you to display keystrokes in manuals, using representative keys, rather than using alternative methods of describing which key to push.

Character Sets

In Chapter 2, you learned that not all fonts have the same characters — certainly Pi fonts have a completely different character set than standard alphanumeric fonts. You discovered that Windows fonts and Macintosh fonts assign different ASCII or ANSI numbers to specific characters, calling for caution when you move jobs cross-platform. You also learned that there are a number of characters on the Windows platform that do not occur on the Macintosh, and vice-versa.

Expert Character Sets

In addition, there are sets of characters that add functionality to the standard keyboard set. Expert character sets exist for some fonts; some have Alternate character sets; others have Small Caps and Oldstyle Figures.

Expert Character Sets contain small caps as the lowercase letters, and use Oldstyle numbers instead of the standard number set.

$$1234567890 \longleftarrow \text{Baseline}$$

$$1234567890 \longleftarrow \text{Baseline}$$

Some Oldstyle number characters dip below the baseline, giving the document a more elegant look, and blending better with lowercase letters in body text.

In addition, they contain common fractions, standard ligatures and a set of superior and baseline-established small numbers for the purpose of constructing fractions. The slash character / is replaced by a vinculum /, which is the correct character to use when constructing piece fractions (this character is available in standard character sets on the Macintosh as Option-Shift-1). Some other characters are also included, bringing the Macintosh and Windows environments closer together.

$$\tfrac14 \ \tfrac12 \ \tfrac34 \ \tfrac18 \ \tfrac38 \ \tfrac58 \ \tfrac78 \ \tfrac13 \ \tfrac23 \quad \text{ff fi fl ffi ffl}$$

$$1234567890 \ / \ 1234567890$$

Fractions, ligatures and the characters needed to build piece fractions are included in Expert character sets.

Summary

In this chapter you have reviewed the historic evolution of type styles, and have explored the characteristics of the various categories of type. In addition, you learned that there are a number of categorization systems. Hopefully, you will be able not only to recognize different categories of type, but also to make decisions about the ways you use type, based on your new knowledge.

SECTION 2

TYPOGRAPHY

You may think that I exaggerate the importance of good typography. You may ask if I have ever heard a housewife say that she bought a new detergent because the advertisement was set in Caslon. No. But do you think an advertisement can sell if nobody can read it? As Mies van der Rohe said of architecture, "God is in the details."

— DAVID OGILVY, *OGILVY ON ADVERTISING*

We live and work in an era of inexpensive and available type. As a result, type is ubiquitous. However, type used well is a different issue entirely. As important as type is to design, its primary purpose is to be read, conveying the writer's message. It is not, as some suggest, to serve simply as a design device.

When you work with type, you must understand its elements. While selection of a typeface is important, selecting an appropriate size and weight are even more so. Headlines that are too big and bold can overpower the text, and may even be unreadable at a normal reading distance. Text that is too small not only loses its character (for example, the serifs or thin strokes may disappear), but is also rendered unreadable. The shape of type also adds to readability. For this reason, we will usually set type in sentence case using the roman (nonitalic, nonbold) font of the family.

Paying attention to details such as alignment and leading makes type more readable and enhances the design of the page overall. Closely related and equally important to readability is the length of the line. The way pages are laid out also contributes to readability, so care should be taken when determining the number of columns per page, the width of columns and gutters, and the width of page margins.

Type's color, or apparent grayness, is another factor that influences the readability and design. The page should appear to have the same density overall to be most pleasing. When type is placed on a colored background, the difference in reflectivity must be taken into account in order to ensure that the type is readable. Devices that may be good design but diminish the usefulness of the text should be avoided.

In order to create good typography, it is important to use typographic characters. When using a typewriter, you can only access characters that exist on the keyboard. Computers allow you to access twice as many characters, such as "real" quotation marks, copyright symbol (©) and more. When the proper symbol is used, documents look much more professional.

Properly setting type to work with rules and in bulleted or numbered lists is an art. When properly constructed, they enhance understanding of the document and add artistic flavor to the pages. When constructed incorrectly, they look bad and are difficult to use — especially if the document is edited.

This sounds like a lot of rules or guidelines, and some may object to the constraints on their creativity. If you feel that way, remember Shakespeare wrote his sonnets within a strict discipline — 14 lines of iambic pentameter rhyming in 3 quatrains and a couplet. Mozart wrote sonatas within an equally rigid discipline — exposition, development and recapitulation. Would any of us say that Shakespeare and Mozart were boring or not creative?

It isn't enough to simply understand the elements of type. Type must be controlled within documents, from properly selecting the fonts to managing the way the type will act within the document.

This includes managing the hyphenation and justification routines, so that a minimum amount of operator intervention is needed to achieve a good-looking result. However, when creating some documents, such as ads or annual reports, overriding the automatic results manually is often necessary. This is where knowledge of the possible, mixed with artistry, makes a difference, and allows the typographer to produce a superior document.

Depending upon the program you use, type can be aligned automatically on the page both horizontally and vertically, and space can be added in a number of ways. Alternately, you can use the page-layout program's baseline grid to aid in positioning type on the page. Closely related to alignment is control of paragraph breaks, termed "widow and orphan control." The ability to keep a specific number of lines together, or even with next paragraphs, is important when document production must be accomplished quickly and accurately.

Use of style sheets makes production fast, accurate and consistent. Most important, it allows separation of editorial and design, with editorial determining the importance of elements and design determining how each element will look.

When you have completed this section, you will understand that while it is important to follow guidelines — and even rules, sometimes — those constraints allow you to produce a better, more consistent document of high quality. You can put your layout program to work to exercise the most control over the document with the least amount of work on your part — freeing you to use your time to concentrate on design.

CHAPTER 4

Understanding the Elements of Type

As we have seen, there are substantial differences in the design of typefaces. Many of those differences jump out at us, but others lie in elements that are not obvious as we look at a character set or at a composed headline. Typefaces with hundreds or thousands of kerning pairs built in are far easier to work with than fonts with few or no kerning pairs, which we often see in fonts distributed as shareware.

While type is, assuredly, a design element, its primary contribution to the work is the written message it carries. So, while selecting a headline face is fun, ensuring that the body text can be easily read is even more important. In this chapter, we will learn how to ensure that your typeset message receives the attention it deserves, concentrating on its readability. We will see how combining type with rules (lines) can set type off, and how those rules should be applied. We will also explore means to control type within a document.

In order to proceed, we are making certain assumptions: that you are working in a composition program that allows you to control various routines, and that you are familiar with your program. While we will show menus that illustrate specific points, we recognize that not all programs are alike. Some programs will name their functions differently; for example, some may use the term "Space Before" while others will use "Space Above."

The Readability of Type

Type may be readable — or not — based on far more than the typeface you select. Clearly a selection of a heavy font for small body text will make it hard to read. Other factors must also be considered: type size, line length, leading, weight, color (such as cyan), letterspace, capitalization and justification. We will review these factors and more in this section.

Serif vs. Sans-serif Type

There is an ongoing debate concerning the comparative readability of these classes of type. Studies show that, all other factors being equal, there is little difference in the legibility, although serif faces tend to be more readable in long, sustained text. The reason for this is that serifs provide a horizontal flow. That having been said, those who learned to read using serif type have a preference for serif typefaces, while those who learned to read sans-serif type prefer to read sans-serif typefaces. Let's look at a few fonts and compare them. All type will be set in a comparable point size, with comparable line spacing.

> Typography combines the art of the designer with the science of computer technology. Its beauty lies in both its form and execution; so, long after the type is designed, still other designers and technicians are required to take full advantage of its features. – *New Baskerville*
>
> Typography combines the art of the designer with the science of computer technology. Its beauty lies in both its form and execution; so, long after the type is designed, still other designers and technicians are required to take full advantage of its features. – *Neu Helvetica 55*
>
> Typography combines the art of the designer with the science of computer technology. Its beauty lies in both its form and execution; so, long after the type is designed, still other designers and technicians are required to take full advantage of its features. – *Weiss Roman*
>
> Typography combines the art of the designer with the science of computer technology. Its beauty lies in both its form and execution; so, long after the type is designed, still other designers and technicians are required to take full advantage of its features. – *Avant Garde Book*
>
> Typography combines the art of the designer with the science of computer technology. Its beauty lies in both its form and execution; so, long after the type is designed, still other designers and technicians are required to take full advantage of its features. – *Bodoni Regular*

Are any of these typefaces more readable than others? Of course! But the readability is not determined by whether or not the font has serifs. X-height, weight, relationship between thick and thin strokes, and the overall letterform are far more important considerations.

Once we're over the hurdle of selecting serif or sans-serif type, we should concern ourselves with the feel of the type on the page. This is determined in large part by the weight of the type.

Weight

You know by now that type is designed to impart a specific feel to the document. We'll explore here how the weight of type — its thickness or thinness — affects its readability and its effectiveness in communications.

25 Helvetica Neu Ultra Light	Goudy Oldstyle
35 Helvetica NeuThin	**Goudy Bold**
45 Helvetica Neu Light	**Goudy Extrabold**
55 Helvetica Neu Roman	**Goudy Heavyface**
65 Helvetica Neu Medium	Cheltenham Light
75 Helvetica Neu Bold	Cheltenham Book
85 Helvetica Neu Heavy	**Cheltenham Bold**
95 Helvetica Neu Black	**Cheltenham Ultra**

Helvetica Neu runs the full gamut of weights, beginning with 25 (Ultra Light) through 95 (Black). Goudy and ITC Cheltenham also have a variety of weights. Note how their serifs are affected as they become bolder. Here, they are set in 14 pt.

When a very thin typeface is set in a small size, it breaks up, the strokes becoming too light to be printed. When a heavy typeface is set too small, it fills in, rendering the letters unreadable.

Typography combines the art of the designer with the science of computer technology. Its beauty lies in both its form and execution; so, long after the type is designed, still other designers and technicians are required to take full advantage of its features.
– 35 Helvetica Neu Thin, 6/7.5

Typography combines the art of the designer with the science of computer technology. Its beauty lies in both its form and execution; so, long after the type is designed, still other designers and technicians are required to take full advantage of its features.
– 35 Helvetica Neu Thin, 8/9.5

Typography combines the art of the designer with the science of computer technology. Its beauty lies in both its form and execution; so, long after the type is designed, still other designers and technicians are required to take full advantage of its features.
– 45 Helvetica Neu Black, 6/7.5

Typography combines the art of the designer with the science of computer technology. Its beauty lies in both its form and execution; so, long after the type is designed, still other designers and technicians are required to take full advantage of its features.
– 45 Helvetica Neu Black 8/9.5

Typography combines the art of the designer with the science of computer technology. Its beauty lies in both its form and execution; so, long after the type is designed, still other designers and technicians are required to take full advantage of its features.
– Goudy Oldstyle, 6/7.5

Typography combines the art of the designer with the science of computer technology. Its beauty lies in both its form and execution; so, long after the type is designed, still other designers and technicians are required to take full advantage of its features.
– Goudy Oldstyle, 8/9.5

Typography combines the art of the designer with the science of computer technology. Its beauty lies in both its form and execution; so, long after the type is designed, still other designers and technicians are required to take full advantage of its features.
– Goudy Heavyface, 6/7.5

Typography combines the art of the designer with the science of computer technology. Its beauty lies in both its form and execution; so, long after the type is designed, still other designers and technicians are required to take full advantage of its features.
– Goudy Heavyface 8/9.5

When fine type is set to small sizes, it becomes hard to read. Sometime thin strokes break up when they are set in small sizes, such as 6 pt. or below. When using very heavy type, a different problem presents itself: letters tend to fill in. Even at 8 pt., these heavy weights are only marginally readable.

This would lead us to believe that such typefaces should be used in only large sizes. In fact, type set 14 pt. or larger is considered display type, although some department-store ads will use a thin typeface as text in type as large as 24 pt. in a full-page ad. Use of typefaces such as Goudy Heavyface in very large sizes can overpower a page, but their weight can be lessened if they are set in a color other than black.

We will explore the weight of type more in our upcoming discussion about the color of type.

Case

Sometimes we'll see a document with large passages in CAPITAL letters, or SMALL CAPS will be used extensively. The idea, of course, is that the use of these devices enhances readability. In fact, just the opposite occurs.

When in school, we learned to read using both uppercase and lowercase letters. It is not surprising that the use of capital letters only for the first letter of proper nouns, abbreviations and the beginning of the sentence, coupled with the use of miniscules (uncapitalized) letters for everything else, is called "sentence case." A mixture of capital and miniscule letters has greater variety; their form is more recognizable.

typography TYPOGRAPHY

The outline around each word shows how our eye perceives it. It is readily apparent that the shape of the word in lowercase letters has more variety, hence better recognition.

When larger passages of type are set in all caps, they become very hard to read. Instead of emphasizing the text, those who rely on this device simply emphasize their bad taste and lack of understanding of written communication.

Typography combines the art of the designer with the science of computer technology. Its beauty lies in both its form and execution; so, long after the type is designed, still other designers and technicians are required to take full advantage of its features.

TYPOGRAPHY COMBINES THE ART OF THE DESIGNER WITH THE SCIENCE OF COMPUTER TECHNOLOGY. ITS BEAUTY LIES IN BOTH ITS FORM AND EXECUTION; SO, LONG AFTER THE TYPE IS DESIGNED, STILL OTHER DESIGNERS AND TECHNICIANS ARE REQUIRED TO TAKE FULL ADVANTAGE OF ITS FEATURES.

TYPOGRAPHY COMBINES THE ART OF THE DESIGNER WITH THE SCIENCE OF COMPUTER TECHNOLOGY. ITS BEAUTY LIES IN BOTH ITS FORM AND EXECUTION; SO, LONG AFTER THE TYPE IS DESIGNED, STILL OTHER DESIGNERS AND TECHNICIANS ARE REQUIRED TO TAKE FULL ADVANTAGE OF ITS FEATURES.

As you see in this example, the type in all caps assaults our eyes. Small caps are little better — essentially they are just a smaller version. Their size, however, causes the lines to have more space between them, visually making them slightly less uncomfortable.

Does this mean we should never use caps and small caps? No. Occasional use may be indicated, for short passages of text. Using small caps to lead into an article is effective. Some fonts are designed with only capital letters and should not be used for running text.

> TYPOGRAPHY COMBINES THE ART of the designer with the science of computer technology. Its beauty lies in both its form and execution; so, long after the type is designed, still other designers and technicians are required to take full advantage of its features.

The run-in line using small caps is a device often used in newspapers and magazines.

Another good application of small caps is their use in acronyms and for some abbreviations. This, of course, is a matter of a company's preferred style, as is the use of oldstyle figures.

| Cleopatra committed suicide in 31 BC, either by taking poison, or — as the story goes — by the bite of an asp. Egypt subsequently became a Roman province. | Cleopatra committed suicide in 31 BC, either by taking poison, or — as the story goes — by the bite of an asp. Egypt subsequently became a Roman province. |
| The world of DTP is filled with jargon. When you speak of color, you can't escape RGB, CMYK, HSV, or PMS. The files are compressed with LZW, GIF, or JPEG, and we have to watch our LPI, SPI, and DPI. | The world of DTP is filled with jargon. When you speak of color, you can't escape RGB, CMYK, HSV, or PMS. The files are compressed with LZW, GIF, or JPEG, and we have to watch our LPI, SPI, and DPI. |

The column on the left uses full-size caps and display numbers, while the one on the right uses small caps and oldstyle numbers. Which looks better? It's a matter of taste.

Italics

Italic typefaces are beautiful and are often used effectively in subheads, for captions and for other special treatment. They should not be used, however, for long passages of body text. As a rule, italic typefaces have a greater definition of thick and thin strokes than do their roman counterparts. Coupled with their forward motion, this makes them less readable — even fatiguing — when used for long passages.

> Fourscore and seven years ago, our Fathers brought forth on this continent a new nation, conceived in Liberty, and dedicated to the proposition that all men are created equal.
>
> Now we are engaged in a great civil war, testing whether that nation, or any nation so conceived and so dedicated, can long endure. We are met on a great battle-field of that war. We have come to dedicate a portion of that field, as a final resting place for those who here gave their lives that that nation might live. It is altogether fitting and proper that we should do this.

> *Fourscore and seven years ago, our Fathers brought forth on this continent a new nation, conceived in Liberty, and dedicated to the proposition that all men are created equal.*
>
> *Now we are engaged in a great civil war, testing whether that nation, or any nation so conceived and so dedicated, can long endure. We are met on a great battle-field of that war. We have come to dedicate a portion of that field, as a final resting place for those who here gave their lives that that nation might live. It is altogether fitting and proper that we should do this.*
>
> *But, in a larger sense, we can not dedicate — we can not consecrate — we can not hallow*

When you read this extract from the Gettysburg Address, you see why large blocks of text set in italics are more difficult to read. The typefaces used are Palatino and Palatino Italic, 9/11.

Because of the stylization of italic typefaces, some of the letters can even look similar, leading to more difficult communication.

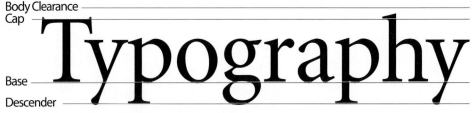

bh bh

The letters b and h look very similar in Sabon Italic (left) and in the varieties of Garamond Italic. Simonici Garamond Italic (right) is shown here.

The mechanics of type also come into play in determining its readability. Type measurement and the measurement of elements on the page are important to the appearance of your document.

Measuring Type

As you learned in Chapter 3, we generally use points and picas to measure type. Type is measured vertically from the base of the descender to the *body clearance line* — a line above the highest point of the tallest glyph — that builds in space between lines of type. Since this "line" is variable space built into the design, typefaces cannot actually be measured vertically.

Body Clearance

Cap

Typography

Base

Descender

The invisible space between the ascender (line not shown) and the body clearance line makes measuring type accurately impossible. This 72-pt. letter measures exactly 72 points from descender to body clearance line.

Adding to our problem of type measurement is the design of typefaces themselves. Each designer has a different idea of how he or she wants the type to appear on a page when set with no additional space between lines.

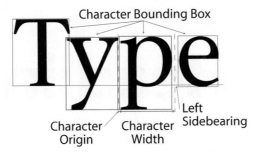

These three typefaces, Helvetica Neu (Linotype Design Staff, 1983), Bodoni Book (Morris Fuller Benton, 1910) and ITC Stone Serif (Sumner Stone, 1987) have substantial differences in their construction. Using Helvetica Neu as a base, both serif faces have a deeper descender and lower cap and x-heights. The ascender of Stone Serif is slightly taller. It is clear that very little interline space is designed into Stone Serif, and that considerable space is allowed above the letters in Bodoni Book. Bodoni Book appears much smaller because of its low x-height.

There is, however, more to measuring type than simply measuring its height. The character width also comes into play. A character has four horizontal measuring elements: Character Origin, Left Sidebearing, Character Bounding Box and Next Character Origin. Taken together, these form the *Character Width*.

The word "Type" above was set using only the kerning built into the typeface. Note that the bounding boxes for the Ty combination overlap, and that there is more space built in between the pe combination.

How does this affect the way we build our pages? The biggest problem that faces page-layout specialists is that of properly handling the Left Sidebearing. The *Left Sidebearing* is space built in between the true Character Origin and the beginning of the Character Bounding Box. Let's see how it affects headlines and paragraphs of text.

Headline

Because the Left Sidebearing is based upon the point size, it is proportionately larger in headlines than it is in body text, giving the impression that the alignment of the headline and the body text is incorrect. To remedy this, it is necessary to physically move the headline to the left in order to align the left margins.

An opposite phenomenon occurs when some italic characters fall against the left margin.

fool your eyes with italics,

Note that the Left sidebearing actually has a minus setting, pushing the character bounding box to the left of the Character Origin point.

From this example, it is clear that we need to take into consideration the mechanical construction of a typeface when we compose our pages.

Generally speaking, the fact that the tail of an italic letter may fall to the left of the text block does not constitute a problem. The inset of large headline characters from the margin, however, constitutes bad typography. It can be overcome in one of two ways:

1. Indent the body text so that the margin is even.

Natural Left Margin →

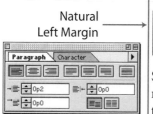

Headline

Since headlines interact with body text, the left margins of both the headline and the block of text must begin at the same point.

We inserted a 2-pt. indent in front of the paragraph to make the left edges of the type align.

2. Create a thin space in front of the headline, and kern until the headline is equal to the left margin.

Natural Left Margin →

Headline

Since headlines interact with body text, the left margins of both the headline and the block of text must begin at the same point.

We inserted a thin space, and then kerned the headline to the space to make the left margins align to the natural margin.

Leading

Measuring the space between lines, often referred to as "line spacing," is called "leading" in typographic terms. There are a number of design rules about leading, many of which conflict with one another. If we keep in mind the maxim "type is to read," we have a basis for making good decisions about the space we place between lines.

Leading is measured from the baseline of one line of type to the baseline above. When type is specified, it is usually described as the point size "over" the leading; 10-pt. type with 12 points of space baseline to baseline is expressed as 10/12. Additional spacing may be added between paragraphs using the Space Before, Space After or Space Between settings. This is sometimes expressed as "plus" leading. So, we would have the specification "Minion Regular, 10/12 +4" to add four points between paragraphs.

The word-processing default is to measure type from ascender to ascender. Adobe PageMaker defaults to proportional spacing — averaging the space between lines rather than using the leading defined if there is a difference in point sizes.

The default leading assigned by most publishing programs is 120% of the point size, but we recommend that, in general, you specify the actual point size and do not use the automatic setting.

The automatic setting is useful when you insert mathematical formulae or in-line graphics into the document. For straight text, you should always specify your leading.

Leading:	12 pt		12 pt
Space Before:	4 pt		4 pt
Space After:	0 pt		0 pt

Leading and interparagraph spacing dialog boxes from the Paragraph Attributes menu (QuarkXPress) and the Character and Paragraph palettes (Adobe InDesign). Interparagraph spacing is additional space inserted before or after paragraphs and is distinct from the leading.

Let's see how this translates into actual blocks of text, using Minion and other typefaces.

10/12 Minion – Typography combines the art of the designer with the science of computer technology. Its beauty lies in both its form and execution; so, long after the type is designed, still other designers and technicians are required to take full advantage of its features.

10/12 Bodoni Book – Typography combines the art of the designer with the science of computer technology. Its beauty lies in both its form and execution; so, long after the type is designed, still other designers and technicians are required to take full advantage of its features.

10/12 New Baskerville – Typography combines the art of the designer with the science of computer technology. Its beauty lies in both its form and execution; so, long after the type is designed, still other designers and technicians are required to take full advantage of its features.

10/12 Stone Sans – Typography combines the art of the designer with the science of computer technology. Its beauty lies in both its form and execution; so, long after the type is designed, still other designers and technicians are required to take full advantage of its features.

Study the blocks of text to determine why they look so different. Could the leading be closed up (decreased) for any of these typefaces? Would you open (increase) it for any of the typefaces? Note that 6 points of interparagraph space has been used to set the copy blocks apart.

Now let's see how varying the leading affects the overall feel of the typeface and its readability. We will use ITC New Baskerville, a font commonly used in book publishing.

10/10 – Typography combines the art of the designer with the science of computer technology. Its beauty lies in both its form and execution; so, long after the type is designed, still other designers and technicians are required to take full advantage of its features.

10/11 – Typography combines the art of the designer with the science of computer technology. Its beauty lies in both its form and execution; so, long after the type is designed, still other designers and technicians are required to take full advantage of its features.

10/12 – Typography combines the art of the designer with the science of computer technology. Its beauty lies in both its form and execution; so, long after the type is designed, still other designers and technicians are required to take full advantage of its features.

10/13 – Typography combines the art of the designer with the science of computer technology. Its beauty lies in both its form and execution; so, long after the type is designed, still other designers and technicians are required to take full advantage of its features.

10/14 – Typography combines the art of the designer with the science of computer technology. Its beauty lies in both its form and execution; so, long after the type is designed, still other designers and technicians are required to take full advantage of its features.

Even in the 10/10 format, ITC New Baskerville is readable because of the built-in body clearance space. It is most readable with more leading, but loses its cohesiveness when the line spacing is exaggerated.

In general, headlines need less leading, as a percentage of the point size, than does text.

Cruise the Caribbean

Spend a glorious 7 days and six nights aboard the all-new cruise ship *Radiance of the Seas*. We'll pamper you with the best in dining, dancing 'til the stars fade, and lounging on deck soaking up the soothing Caribbean sun.

Cruise the Caribbean

Spend a glorious 7 days and six nights aboard the all-new cruise ship *Radiance of the Seas*. We'll pamper you with the best in dining, dancing 'til the stars fade, and lounging on deck soaking up the soothing Caribbean sun.

In this example, the type and headline are both set in Minion Regular. The text is 10/12, a common text setting, and in keeping with the default +20% leading normally assigned by publishing programs. The headline on the left is set 30/22 — a setting of –8 points. (This works because of the absence of descenders.) The headline on the right is 30/36, which is the same percent type size to leading size as the body text. Which looks better to you?

Now that we've discussed vertical measurement, and have a general understanding of how it affects the readability of type, let's see the effect of horizontal measurement.

Line Length

How long should a line of type be? The real answer must be, "it depends." It depends on the typeface being used, the size of type, graphic elements on the page, the justification routines being used, the line spacing, the volume of type and the purpose of the document. In this section, we'll help you apply principles to set acceptable standards.

Normal readers do not read one word at a time; we read groups of words. A line of type should be short enough so that our eyes can read it in one or two jumps, otherwise, the eyes grow tired and have difficulty finding the beginning of the next line. It should be short enough so we are not constantly returning to the beginning of the line, disrupting the sentence structure. As a rule, a line of type should be from 50 to 70 characters in length.

A line of type should generally be from 50 to 70 characters in length.

In general terms, assuming a typeface that is not condensed or expanded, we can say that the minimum line length in picas is about 1.25 times the point size, the optimum about 1.75 and the maximum about 2.5. This assumes a typeface that has between 2.4 and 2.8 characters per pica when using 10-pt. type. If a more condensed typeface is used, a shorter line length should be chosen; a wider face should be set to a longer line length. For example, in the following chart, 6-pt. type has a minimum 7.5-pica line length, an optimum 10.5-pica line length and a maximum 15-pica line length. This conclusion is derived by using the formula:

minimum line length: 6 (points) × 1.25 = 7.5 (picas)

optimum line length: 6 (points) × 1.75 = 10.5 (picas)

maximum line length: 6 (points) × 2.5 = 15 (picas)

Size	Minimum	Optimum	Maximum
6	7.5	10.5	15
7	8.75	12.25	17.5
8	10	14	20
9	11.25	15.75	22.5
10	12.5	17.5	25
11	13.75	19.25	27.5
12	15	21	30
14	17.5	24.5	35
16	20	28	40

This chart gives generic minimum, optimum and maximum line lengths, based on the guidelines given in the preceding paragraph. Fonts with narrower widths should be set to shorter line lengths, while wider-setting fonts should be set to a longer line length.

When type is set to longer line lengths or has a large x-height, it should be given additional leading, to allow the eye to read it more easily.

Typography combines the art of the designer with the science of computer technology. Its beauty lies in both its form and execution; so, long after the type is designed, still other designers and technicians are required to take full advantage of its features.

Typography combines the art of the designer with the science of computer technology. Its beauty lies in both its form and execution; so, long after the type is designed, still other designers and technicians are required to take full advantage of its features.

Typography combines the art of the designer with the science of computer technology. Its beauty lies in both its form and execution; so, long after the type is designed, still other designers and technicians are required to take full advantage of its features.

Typography combines the art of the designer with the science of computer technology. Its beauty lies in both its form and execution; so, long after the type is designed, still other designers and technicians are required to take full advantage of its features.

ITC Cheltenham Light has a relatively large x-height. The first paragraph uses a standard 10/12 setting and is a little tight. We increased the leading to 10/13.5 in the second paragraph, for a notable improvement in readability. Using ITC Cheltenham Condensed Light, even the increased leading was insufficient to make the type read easily. We decreased the line length from 25 picas to 20 picas, for an acceptable result. (The character count in 10-pt. type for each face is: ITC Cheltenham, 2.75; ITC Cheltenham Condensed 3.46.)

In addition, typefaces with strong thick and thin strokes need to be set to shorter line lengths than fonts whose strokes are more regular, in order to avoid a "picket fence" look.

Typography combines the art of the designer with the science of computer technology. Its beauty lies in both its form and execution; so, long after the type is designed, still other designers and technicians are required to take full advantage of its features.

Typography combines the art of the designer with the science of computer technology. Its beauty lies in both its form and execution; so, long after the type is designed, still other designers and technicians are required to take full advantage of its features.

Typography combines the art of the designer with the science of computer technology. Its beauty lies in both its form and execution; so, long after the type is designed, still other designers and technicians are required to take full advantage of its features.

Bodoni Roman (used in the top two text blocks) has strong thick and thin strokes. It looks much better set to a line length of 21 picas than it does set to the 25-pica length. Palatino, with more even stroke weights, is set to the full 25-pica line length.

Your line length is determined ultimately by the page size, and how you design the text area of that document. Our next section will help you apply design skills to maximize the appearance of text on the page.

Justification (Alignment)

When text aligns to a margin, it is said to be "justified," "aligned" or "flush" to that margin. When we speak of *justified text*, we normally mean that it is flush to both left and right margins — or to specified indents from those margins. Justified text, when properly set, is easy to read. When improperly set it becomes difficult to read, developing unsightly rivers of white that affect the overall look of the block of text.

A river is a wide area of white running through a column of type.

Text that aligns to either the left or right margin is termed "left justified," "right justified," "flush left" or "flush right." Sometimes people refer to the opposite margin — the unjustified edge — as "ragged right" or "ragged left." In both cases, the appearance of the ragged edge must be controlled carefully. Text with deep "rags" becomes very hard to read. The advantage of setting type with a ragged edge is that there is equal spacing between every word, enhancing its readability.

Type set flush left can contain hyphens, but they should be infrequent. This setting has become the setting of choice for many types of documents.

Type set flush right is hard to read, because there is no solid margin to which the eye can return. It should be used sparingly, for specific purposes, such as figure captions. It should never contain hyphens.

Text that is ragged on both edges is said to be "set centered" or "ragged both." Centered text is hard to read in large blocks, but looks elegant for invitations and some headlines.

Typography combines the art of the designer with the science of computer technology. Its beauty lies in both its form and execution; so, long after the type is designed, still other designers and technicians are required to take full advantage of its features.

Typography combines the art of the designer with the science of computer technology. Its beauty lies in both its form and execution; so, long after the type is designed, still other designers and technicians are required to take full advantage of its features.

Typography combines the art of the designer with the science of computer technology. Its beauty lies in both its form and execution; so, long after the type is designed, still other designers and technicians are required to take full advantage of its features.

Typography combines the art of the designer with the science of computer technology. Its beauty lies in both its form and execution; so, long after the type is designed, still other designers and technicians are required to take full advantage of its features.

Attention to detail is needed, regardless of what justification routine is selected. We want to avoid unsightly rivers of type or ragged type that has too much or too little variation in line length.

Margins and Columns

Whether you're designing a quarter-page ad or a multivolume series of books, you need to consider not just the space that the type and graphics will occupy, but also the surrounding white space.

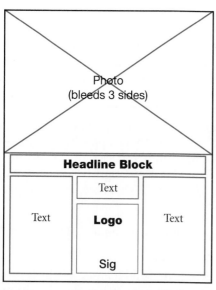

In this mockup of a magazine advertisement, the top half of the page is taken up by the photograph. A headline block follows; text is presented in three columns. The logo and related information are at the bottom of the center column. In an ad such as this, it is important to allow enough marginal space and space between columns so that the type is easy to read. The completed ad is to the right.

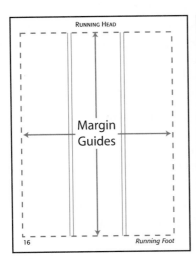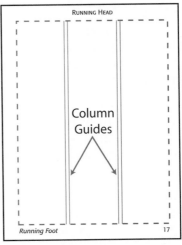

This typical three-column grid allows extra space for the inside margins. This would be particularly important if there were many pages, or if the publication were to be punched for loose-leaf binding. Notice that adequate room has been left for running head and feet.

The most fundamental rule about margins and intercolumnar space (sometimes called "gutters") is that you must leave adequate space so the type does not appear cramped on the page, and so that columns of type do not run into one another. When you're producing a document like a book, you must also ensure that there is enough inside margin space so that type next to that margin can be read after the book is bound. Of course, it's also necessary to keep type away from the outside margins. You can't print to the edge of the page — or even too near it, because trimming is a mechanical function, only accurate to approximately $1/32''$.

Working with your design grid enables you to set up a variety of formats for your page, keeping in mind the information we discussed earlier about line lengths relative to the size of the type you are using. Assume you are working with a 7-in. by 9-in. page size, and the type size is 11 pt. Keeping within the parameters, what options can you create?

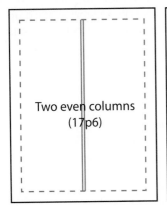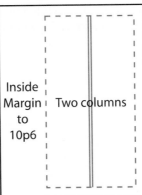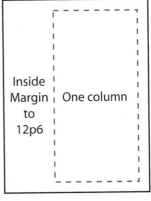

These are the primary designs available for a 7-in. × 9-in. page design for a book. Of course, graphics can be added, breaking up the somewhat rigid design grid.

Columns per Page

Occasionally, we hear of design rules concerning the maximum number of columns that should be used per page. While the line-length rule is a primary factor, you would usually want to make your columns wider rather than narrower. Narrow columns cause more hyphenation and more bad line breaks than occur with wider columns.

While three columns is pretty much the maximum for text on a letter-size page, you can do five columns in 10-pt. type, and six columns in moderately narrow-setting 9-pt. or smaller type. You can also break up the number of columns, when working on documents like magazines and newspapers, combining two or three columns into one for featured elements.

Remember, too, that columns often hold information other than running text. They are used extensively in financial reports, so the number of characters in the column may be very few, and the type might be relatively small.

Combining the elements we've talked about so far brings us to the overall appearance of type on the page. This is called the type's "color."

Color

The *color* of type is the apparent grayness of a paragraph or group of paragraphs. With the exception of headlines, pull quotes and illustrations, we want the page to appear to be a consistent shade of gray. This color can be interrupted by bad letter- and word-spacing, bad hyphenation, inattention to the raggedness of paragraphs or justified lines, irregular leading and improper use of different weights of type. The overall darkness or lightness of the color can be affected by the choice of typeface.

> **Pull quotes are extracts "pulled" from the document and treated very much like artwork.**

To properly manage the color of your type, pay careful attention to such details as justification and the raggedness of lines. If you need to track type to work a word up or down, try tracking the entire paragraph so words in one or two lines won't be jammed together.

ALICE was beginning to get very tired of sitting by her sister on the bank, and of having nothing to do: once or twice she had peeped into the book her sister was reading, but it had no pictures or conversations in it, "and what is the use of a book," thought Alice, "without pictures or conversation?"

So she was considering in her own mind (as well as she could, for the hot day made her feel very sleepy and stupid) whether the pleasure of making a daisy-chain would be worth the trouble of getting up and picking the daisies, when suddenly a White Rabbit with pink eyes ran close by.

There was nothing so very remarkable in that; nor did Alice think it so very much out of the way to hear the Rabbit say to itself, "Oh dear! Oh dear! I shall be too late!" (when she thought it over afterwards, it occurred to her that she ought to have wondered at this, but at the time it all seemed quite natural); but when the Rabbit actually took a watch out of its waist-coat pocket, and looked at it, and then hurried on, Alice started to her feet, for it flashed across her mind that she had never before seen a rabbit with either a waist-coat pocket or a watch to take out of it, and burning with curiosity, she ran across the field after it, and fortunately was just in time to see it pop down a large rabbit-hole under the hedge.

In another moment down

Can you identify the elements that break up the even color in this sample? Try turning the page upside down and holding it at a distance. You should find one problem in each column.

When inserting an in-line graphic, try to size it so that it will fit within the leading for that paragraph. This is one reason why it's best to specify your leading in points rather than using auto leading. When auto leading is used, your program may increase the leading a point or two to accommodate the in-line graphic. This would create unevenness in the overall color of type, and type would not align across the page.

Sometimes it is useful to insert graphics into the text stream. This is sometimes done when describing icons in a textbook. In-line graphics, such as the one at the end of this paragraph, are sometimes used to signify the end of an article.

You will also want to avoid using passages of italics or bold type, particularly when the italics are appreciably lighter than the roman face being used for body text.

In another moment down went Alice after it, never once considering how in the world she was to get out again.

The rabbit-hole went straight on like a **tunnel** for some way, and then dipped suddenly down, *so suddenly that Alice had not a moment to think about stopping herself before she found herself falling* down a very deep well.

Either the well was very deep, or she fell very slowly, for she had plenty of time as *she went down to look about her, and to wonder what was going to happen next.* First, she tried to look down and make out what she was coming to, but it was too dark to **see** anything; then she looked at the sides of the well, and noticed that they were filled with **cupboards** and **book-shelves**: here and there she saw maps and pictures hung upon pegs. She took down a **jar** from one of the shelves as she passed; it was labelled **Orange Marmalade**, but to her great disappointment it was empty: she did not like to drop the jar for fear of **killing** somebody, so managed to put it into one of the cupboards as she fell past it.

The passages of italics and spotty boldface ruin the color of this sample of text.

You can, however, use the weight of type to give your text a tone. This is most easily accomplished using typefaces that have a good variety of weights, such as Helvetica Neu or ITC Garamond.

"CURIOUSER and curiouser!" cried Alice (she was so much surprised, that for the moment she quite forgot how to speak good English); "now I'm opening out like the largest telescope that ever was! Good-bye, feet!" (for when she looked down at her feet, they seemed to be almost out of sight, they were getting so far off). "Oh, my poor little feet, I wonder who will put on your shoes and stockings for you now, dears? I'm sure I shan't be able! I shall be a great deal too far off to trouble myself about you: you must manage the best way you can—but I must be kind to

"CURIOUSER and curiouser!" cried Alice (she was so much surprised, that for the moment she quite forgot how to speak good English); "now I'm opening out like the largest telescope that ever was! Good-bye, feet!" (for when she looked down at her feet, they seemed to be almost out of sight, they were getting so far off). "Oh, my poor little feet, I wonder who will put on your shoes and stockings for you now, dears? I'm sure I shan't be able! I shall be a great deal too far off to trouble myself about you: you must manage the best way you can—but I must be kind to them," thought Alice, "or per-

Note how the difference in weight between ITC Garamond Light and Book changes the effect of the text. Interestingly, the Book weight is designed with a notably narrower width, and has a greater number of characters per pica than the Light weight.

Generally speaking, type that is light and airy is easier to read than type that is heavier. In the example we show, ITC Garamond Light is more inviting to read than the heavier Book weight.

Black, White and Gray Type

A typeface's readability is diminished whenever it is presented in a form other than black type on a white page. The worst application in common use is to set body-sized type reversed out of a background — white on black or another color. The worst possible case is body type reversed out of a process-color image. Even the slightest misregistration on press can result in unreadable type.

Registration *is the process of properly aligning colors on a printing press. When misregistration occurs, the result is a fuzzy image.*

To effectively communicate your ideas, remember, type is to read.
To effectively communicate your ideas, remember, type is to read.
To effectively communicate your ideas, remember, type is to read.
To effectively communicate your ideas, remember, type is to read.
To effectively communicate your ideas, remember, type is to read.
To effectively communicate your ideas, remember, type is to read.
To effectively communicate your ideas, remember, type is to read.
To effectively communicate your ideas, remember, type is to read.
To effectively communicate your ideas, remember, type is to read.
To effectively communicate your ideas, remember, type is to read.
To effectively communicate your ideas, remember, type is to read.
To effectively communicate your ideas, remember, type is to read.

When selecting backgrounds, whether they are a photograph, a color or a tint, remember that in order to communicate effectively, the type must be easily readable.

6-point 55 Helvetica Neu Roman. Setting reversed type at small sizes — even when the typeface would normally be readable at that size — is a bad idea. The art of communication is not the ability to torture your readers, but to make the process of reading your message enjoyable.

6-point 65 Helvetica Neu Medium. Note how much easier the Medium weight of this font is to read than the Roman, or Book weight. If at all possible, you want to avoid giving your reader blocks of small, reversed type to read. At the very least, you would want to use a shorter line length.

6-point Goudy Oldstyle. Even though some typefaces can stand up to the abuses of being set in a very small size and reversed, type with elegant serifs disintigrates when subjected to this treatment. The serifs and thin strokes of this typeface virtually disappear at this size.

Even when set at 12 point, the serifs and thin strokes of Goudy Oldstyle are in jeopardy, if the printing isn't nearly perfect.

Ideally, reversed type, when it must be used, will be set sans-serif, with adequate size, weight, and leading, such as this typeface, Futura Medium.

Even when type is reversed out of a solid background, take care to ensure that your type is large enough to read, and that its letterform will stand up to being reversed.

We see major abuses of type on Web pages. Type that is pure blue (0000FF) is often reversed out of a black background, creating a click-on-another-page scenario because it is hard on the eyes. Type and the Web will be discussed in more detail in Chapter 6.

Another type abuse is the design device of using gray ink instead of black. If the gray is dark enough, it simply looks like washed-out black. At other times, when a light gray is used, the type can disappear into the background.

Tracking and Kerning

We mentioned earlier in this chapter that well-designed typefaces have many built-in kerning pairs. Even so, when creating display text, tracking and kerning are almost always needed. There is an almost overpowering temptation on the part of many to overkern and overtrack type.

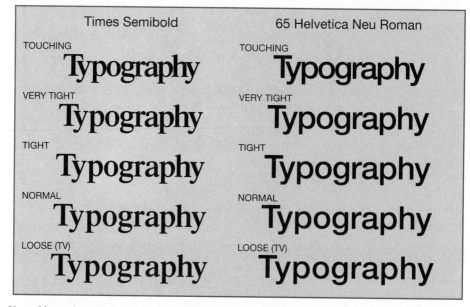

Tracking tables such as this have been in use for years.

TV Tracking is so-named because type expands on television since light is transmitted rather than reflected.

When tracking — especially when tracking body text — resist the temptation to track tightly. The letters must have enough room for their shape to interact properly with the letters around them. Overtracking can result in text that is difficult to read, just as text that is too loose causes the eyes to have to work harder to combine the letters into words.

Tracking adjusts the spacing across a range of characters, and should be approached on a paragraph-by-paragraph basis to achieve a consistent color on the page. Kerning adjusts the spacing between two adjacent letters, or between a letter and a space.

We the People of the United States, in Order to form a more perfect Union, establish Justice, insure domestic Tranquility, provide for the common defence, promote the general Welfare, and secure the Blessings of Liberty to ourselves and our Posterity, do ordain and establish this Constitution for the United States of America.

We the People of the United States, in Order to form a more perfect Union, establish Justice, insure domestic Tranquility, provide for the common defence, promote the general Welfare, and secure the Blessings of Liberty to ourselves and our Posterity, do ordain and establish this Constitution for the United States of America.

We the People of the United States, in Order to form a more perfect Union, establish Justice, insure domestic Tranquility, provide for the common defence, promote the general Welfare, and secure the Blessings of Liberty to ourselves and our Posterity, do ordain and establish this Constitution for the United States of America.

We the People of the United States, in Order to form a more perfect Union, establish Justice, insure domestic Tranquility, provide for the common defence, promote the general Welfare, and secure the Blessings of Liberty to ourselves and our Posterity, do ordain and establish this Constitution for the United States of America.

In this sample, which uses Palatino Roman, 10/12 and a line length of 25 picas, we tracked the first paragraph very tightly, the second tightly, the third normally and the fourth loosely. Note the difference in readability.

When you kern and track headlines, the best way to work with the letters is to kern to white space, rather than paying attention to the letters themselves. When display text is properly kerned, the white space appears consistent: no letter pair is too close or too distant from one another. To evaluate headline spacing, step away and squint at the type — or turn it upside down. You should see an evenness of gray tone. If you see spots that are too light or too dark, the letters are too close to or too distant from one another.

Come over the
mountains and drink in
our valleys.

NAPA-SONOMA
WINE ASSOCIATION

This combination of round typefaces — ITC Avant Garde Gothic and University Roman — is an interesting choice. The headline is heavily tracked. Because of the type design, no letter pairs were kerned. NAPA-SONOMA, however, presented a challenge. The MA letter pair determined the overall tightness of the words, because to kern them more tightly would overlap the letters, which we did not want to do.

Special Characters

As you have already learned, there's a remarkable difference between typography and simply typing letters onto a page. One of the biggest differences is proper use of typographic characters — characters that print as well as those used for spacing.

Quotes and Related Characters

While the typewriter keyboard constrains us to using only the prime and double prime, our computers give us access to quotation marks, apostrophes and inch marks, as well.

" " ' '	Quotation Marks, double (outside) and single (inside)
'	Apostrophe
" '	Inch and Foot marks
‖	Ditto and Prime

There are obvious differences between these marks, and a good typographer uses them all correctly.

Quotation marks. Quotation marks may be used in either double or single form. They are used to enclose the exact words of a speaker or writer. Usually, the opening marks are weighted to the bottom and the closing marks are weighted to the top, but this is not always the case; it is a decision made by the type designer.

In general practice in the United States, double quotation marks are used for a standard quotation, and single quotation marks are used for a quote within a quote. If the inner quotation ends the sentence, then a thin space should be inserted between the inner and outer quotes. For example, Erin said, "The Gettysburg Address begins 'Fourscore and seven years ago.'"

> **When you end a sentence with an inner quotation, be sure to insert a thin space between the inner and outer quotation marks.**

In the United State, a period (.) or comma (,) always falls inside the quotes. Other punctuation falls inside or outside the quote, depending upon whether it is part of the quotation or not.

Apostrophe. An apostrophe is used to indicate that a portion of the word is missing (as in the words "don't" or "can't"), or to indicate possession (Pat's shillelagh collection). When used in front of a year, such as '01, it must be manually inserted; "smart quote" routines will insert the single open quote instead of the apostrophe.

Inch and foot marks. These marks are used to denote inches and seconds or feet and minutes, respectively. While they are part of the standard character set under Windows, they must be accessed from Symbol, Universal or another Pi font on the Macintosh.

Hyphens and Dashes

When the typewriter was used for correspondence, either a hyphen (-) or a double hyphen (--) would be used in all instances where hyphens and dashes came into play. With the availability of typographic dashes, it is important to know when each should be used.

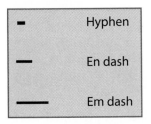

Note the different lengths of dashes. Each has its specific use.

Hyphen. A hyphen is used to tie words together. When a word is too long to fit on a line, the hyphen ties the letters on the first line with the balance of the word. It also ties compound words together, such as "re-create," "long-lived" or "two-year-old."

> **Because "recreate" means to refresh by play or amusement, the hyphen is needed when using the term re-create, meaning "to make again," differentiating the two words.**

Most composition programs allow you to enter a discretionary hyphen, which creates a hyphen at that point in the word only if the word does not fit on a line. A discretionary hyphen placed in front of a word forces the word to not hyphenate. A non-breaking hyphen can also be inserted. A non-breaking hyphen causes the word in which it is placed to fall to the following line as a unit, rather than breaking at the hyphen.

En dash. An en dash is used to replace the word "to" or "through." It is used to separate words in a phrase, such as "December 15–January 2." Spaces should not be used with an en dash, but a thin space is often desirable, to keep it from touching the characters on either side. The en dash is also used to represent the minus sign in mathematical expressions. He set the tracking to –5.

Em dash. An em dash is used to separate word groups within a sentence. "Type may be readable — or may be difficult to read — depending upon the typeface you select." They act as parentheses, but with more authority. No

> *While "no space around em dashes" is the generally accepted rule, house styles vary. The important thing is to be consistent.*

more than a single set of em dashes should be used in a sentence. Like the en dash, justifying spaces should not be used to set the dash apart from other characters.

Special Characters

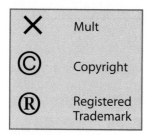

- ✕ Mult
- © Copyright
- ® Registered Trademark

The multiplication sign, copyright and registered trademark symbols should all be used in place of typewritten subsitutes

Multiplication sign. The multiplication sign or mult is a specific character. It is a glyph of the standard character set under Windows, but must be accessed using a Pi font on the Macintosh (such as Symbol). Aside from its mathematical uses, it is also used in architecture (a 15′ × 22′ room) and to define lumber (a 4′ × 8′ sheet of plywood). An ex (x) should never be used in place of the mult.

Copyright symbol. The copyright symbol is used to designate a copyrighted work. The symbol may be used whether or not the work has been registered with the Copyright Office, because copyright is automatically conferred upon the creator of intellectual property, with some limitations. The copyright symbol is a standard character on both Macintosh (Option-g) and Windows (ANSI 0169) computers.

Registered trademark symbol. The registered trademark symbol may be used when a word, phrase or design, used to identify a company, has been registered with the state or with the U.S. Patent and Trademark Office. Unregistered trademarks use the ™ symbol, which may be accessed as a special character or typed. The registered trademark symbol is a standard character on both Macintosh (Option-r) and Windows (ANSI 0174) computers.

Spacing Options

When using a typewriter, we had only two ways to insert a space — we could press the spacebar or press the Tab key. This is also true of most word-processing programs. When composing pages typographically, we need more control over spacing, and page-layout programs give us that control. Not all of the options we mention are available in all page-layout programs, however, and those that are available may be accessed by different key combinations.

Non-breaking space. The non-breaking space, like the non-breaking hyphen, is used to keep two words together. For example, you may want to ensure that "St. Louis" always appears as a unit, rather than falling on two lines. A non-breaking space is variable in width when type is justified to both margins.

Em space. The em space is a fixed space the width of the point size. An em in 12-pt. type is 12 points wide; an em in 10-pt. type is 10 points wide.

En space. The en space is a fixed space half the width of an em space.

Thin space. The thin space is a fixed space half the width of an en space.

Flex space. The flex space is a fixed space that may be programmed to any specific width.

> **QuarkXPress bases its spacing on the en and has no dedicated em space. Two en spaces must be inserted instead.**

Fixed spaces are useful because, even when the type is justified to both margins, they will not alter their width.

Paragraph indents should be inserted using the first-line indent function of the word-processing or page-layout program. When they are inserted in this manner, they can be easily changed, if desired.

Combining Type with Rules

Rules, or lines, are used to set elements apart; they are natural eye stoppers. They may be used to box elements or to set apart pull quotes from a body of text. Often they are used between columns or rows in tables. They may also be placed between columns of text to provide a better-defined columnar barrier.

Rules in Columns and Tables

Rules placed between columns of type allow you to use smaller intercolumnar space than would be possible relying on the columns themselves. They are especially useful with a text-intensive document. When inserting rules of this type, you draw the rules with the line tool in your page-layout program.

17th Century

Interested in fishing, trading and lumber, the first colonists came from England. In 1623, they established settlements at Pannaway (Odiorne Point) and Great Island (New Castle). By 1633, the beginnings of the town known as Strawbery Banke were laid out including a grist mill and the Great House, a large communal residence.

In 1653, the inhabitants (about 60 families) petitioned to change the town's name to Portsmouth. New Hampshire was separated as a royal colony from Massachusetts in 1679 and Portsmouth became the capital of the new colonial government. Its first real "building boom" began in 1693 when the Cutts family agreed to subdivide their

farm land around Strawbery Banke into streets and house lots. Streets were narrow and homes were built to the street with yards and outbuildings behind. You might get a feel for this if you walk along the side streets in the Prescott Park area. The town grew rapidly along the waterfront west to present day Market Square and Pleasant Street.

Note how much easier it is to read the text in columns two and three than it is in column one. The vertical rule provides a visual stopping point for your eyes.

Still another application of rules is to make tables more understandable. They may be used for financial data or, as in our example, to define a variety of tables in directories.

RESTAURANTS

KEY ♿ Handicap Accessible ★ Yes ☆ Limited **Rates** $ 0–10 $$ 16–30	Handicap Access	Dates Open	Meals Served	# of Seats	Non-smoking Area	Credit Cards	Avg. Dinner Entrée	Child Menu	Liquor License	Open Air Deck	CUISINE					
											Traditional	Continental	Seafood	Beef	Ethnic	Lighter Fare
ABERCROMBIE & FINCH RESTAURANT 219 Lafayette Rd., N Hampton, NH 03862 603/555-9774	♿	YR	L/D	200	★	★	$–$$		★		★	★	★	★	★	★
ASHWORTH BY THE SEA 295 Ocean Blvd., Hampton Beach, NH 03842 603/555-6762	♿	YR	B/L/D	300	★	★	$$	★	★	★	★	★	★	★	★	★
BANANAS BAR & GRILL 172 Hanover St., Portsmouth, NH 03801 603/555-5795		YR	L/D	230	★	★	$	★	★				★	★		★
GALLEY HATCH RESTAURANT 325 Lafayette Rd., Rte. 1, Hampton, NH 03842 603/555-6152	♿	YR	L/D	440	★	★	$–$$	★	★		★	★	★	★	★	★
THE LOAF AND LADLE 9 Water St., Exeter, NH 03833 603/555-8955	☆	YR	B/L/D	90	★	★	$		★	★	★					★
MOLLY MALONE'S RESTAURANT 177 State St., Portsmouth, NH 03801 603/555-7233	♿	YR	L/D	120	★	★	$$		★				★	★	★	★
THE ROCKINGHAM LIBRARY RESTAURANT 401 State St., Portsmouth, NH 03801 603/555-5202		YR	L/D	100		★	$$		★		★	★	★	★	★	★

Imagine how difficult this chart would be to read without the rules to give it structure.

Rules as Accents

Rules are often used as accents — to make elements stand out from other items on the page. When rules are used in this way they should not be drawn, but should instead be selected from the rules menu, which is usually linked to the paragraph menu. Rules are selected as Rule Above or Rule Below the paragraph. Rules should be of a light enough weight so that they enhance rather than overpower the text.

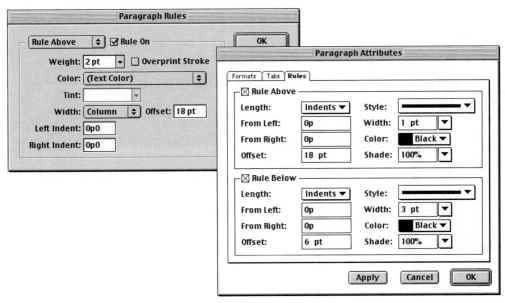

The paragraph rules menus from Adobe InDesign (left) and QuarkXPress (right). To use InDesign's rules, you toggle between the Rule Above and Rule Below menus.

One such use is for callouts from the text, used to reinforce a point made in the text and to add decoration.

INTEGRATED LANGUAGE ARTS

Listening comprehension and reading comprehension are closely related, and story-related speaking and writing activities can lead to improvements in comprehension. So integrating the language arts makes sense.

In *World of Reading*, listening, speaking, and writing activities help students prepare to hear or read a selection and to retell, discuss, and respond to it.

Listening activities include read-aloud/think-aloud selections, listening for specific purposes, and sing-with-me and read-with-me experiences.

Speaking activities include prereading discussions that develop concepts, build background, and set purposes for reading. A Reader's Response question at the end of each story invites students to express a personal reaction. Working Together involves students in cooperative-learning activities.

Writing activities include Writing to Learn comprehension exercises after each selection. The five-step Writing Process at the end of every unit provides readers with an opportunity to express their understanding and response to literature and the unit theme. Writing activities are also included after each vocabulary lesson to help students use story words.

> *"Listening activities include sing-with-me and read-with-me experiences."*

The Teacher Edition offers Language Arts Connections and Curriculum Connections with each story. Language Arts Connections include suggestions such as writing plays, enacting stories, doing interviews, and echo reading. Curriculum Connections are independent activities integrating language arts with social studies, science, math, music, art, and health.

Pull quotes reinforce the message contained in the text.

Closely related to pull quotes or callouts, are quotes from other sources, or other material that may be closely related, but which doesn't fit with the flow of text.

Publishing Systems Audits

Compositors, in-plant operations, printers, service bureaus, publishers and corporations are assisted in the selection of appropriate hardware and software; systems are designed to optimize their hardware and software acquisitions. We work with clients to initiate solutions to specific problems, including those that require implementation of management systems and which affect the manner in which people work.

After having you come to our company our production time has decreased and our profit has increased. I can't thank you enough for your help!

– SS, Philadelphia

Audits review capacity, the utilization of human resources and equipment, based on historical data, present circumstances and projections. They take into consideration our clients' needs and expectations, both long- and short-term.

Because we are an independent consulting group, recommendations are not influenced by potential sales of hardware or software, but are based solely on the needs of our clients.

Set off an advertising message within the text using rules, as was done here.

Rules can also be used to create a headline that is reversed out of a bar, instead of dropping it in as an in-line graphic. Since they are created through the paragraph menu, this treatment can be saved as a paragraph style and applied with the click of a mouse.

Headlines Reverse Out of Rules

Paragraph Attributes			
Formats	Tabs	**Rules**	

☒ **Rule Above**

Length:	Indents ▼	Style:	▼
From Left:	0p	Width:	18 pt ▼
From Right:	0p	Color:	Red ▼
Offset:	-4 pt	Shade:	100% ▼

This headline, created in QuarkXPress, can be applied as a paragraph style, so all of the text and graphic attributes are applied at a single keystroke or mouse click.

Creating Lists

Lists in text are frequently used. Generally speaking, they take three forms: bulleted lists, numbered lists (which might use letters instead of numbers) and unnumbered lists. In almost every case, these lists have commonalities:

1. The elements of the list are treated as separate and distinct from running text. As such, they must be separated from the text so that the list stands apart.

2. Individual elements of the list should be set apart from one another.

3. Because of their nature, lists are usually set flush left, even if the running text of the document is justified.

In order to ensure these points, the list elements should be set apart from running text by additional space. While the list elements should have space between them, that space should be less than the space that separates the list from running text. Indenting the list from the standard margins helps to set it apart further. Reducing the leading in list text may also be useful. List formats should always be saved as styles, to ensure consistency. (Styles will be considered in the next chapter.) There are three styles for every list:

1. The first element in the list, which includes extra space above, offsetting the list from running text.

2. A standard list style, including space above each list item.

3. The last element in the list, which includes space below the item, offsetting the list from running text.

Bulleted Lists

This most-used list consists of a bullet character followed by text. Continuing lines of text should align with the text, not with the bullet character.

To accomplish this, the left indent is set for the entire paragraph, and then a hanging indent (outdent) is set for the bullet character. Some programs require a tab position to be set at the same point as the left indent, while others do not.

Paragraph Attributes

Formats | Tabs | Rules

Left Indent:	2p
First Line:	-1p
Right Indent:	2p
Leading:	13 pt
Space Before:	4 pt
Space After:	0 pt
Alignment:	Left
H&J:	Standard

☐ Drop Caps
Character Count: 1
Line Count: 3

☑ Keep Lines Together
● All Lines in ¶
○ Start: 2 End: 2

☐ Keep with Next ¶
☐ Lock to Baseline Grid

[Apply] [Cancel] [OK]

The Paragraph Attributes menu from QuarkXPress shows indents and spacing for the first bullet item. Succeeding bullet items have a 2-pt. space before; the last item also has a 4-pt. space after.

Experience two days of no-holds-barred discussions with publishing and marketing pros.¶

•→Maximize tools and opportunities to profit from in-house composition¶

•→Learn to design effective documents using your computer¶

•→Understand the ins and outs of color on the desktop¶

•→Design and write compelling brochures and newsletters that get results¶

You won't want to miss this two-day seminar addressing profitable opportunities for publishing, expanded use of desktop technologies in the workplace and tips to make your publications

This is the result of applying the previous settings to text. "Invisibles" showing paragraph endings and tab settings are shown in blue.

Both QuarkXPress and Adobe InDesign have an alternate way to set bulleted text, which is especially useful if the bullet character may change. They use an Indent to Here command. To use this method, simply set up the overall paragraph indent and appropriate space before and after, set the bullet character, space and insert the Indent to Here character. All succeeding lines in the paragraph will align to this new indent.

Experience two days of no-holds-barred discussions with publishing and marketing pros. ¶

- Maximize tools and opportunities to profit from in-house composition ¶
- Learn to design effective documents using your computer ¶
- Understand the ins and outs of color on the desktop ¶
- Design and write compelling brochures and newsletters that get results ¶

You won't want to miss this two-day seminar addressing profitable opportunities for publishing, expanded use of desktop technologies in the workplace and tips to make your publications more effective.

The same text, using the Indent to Here command.

Numbered Lists

The numbered list is similar to the bulleted list, except that it requires an additional tab. The numbered list is set up with a decimal or right-aligning tab so single-digit and double-digit numbers will align preceding the tab needed to align the list text.

Select your course from the following list:
  1. → Desktop Design for the Non-designer
  2. → Desktop Presentations: Simple & Sensational
  3. → Training Solutions and Strategic Alliances
  4. → How to Put Illustration Programs to Work
 10. → The Good, the Bad, and the Unprintable
 11. → Matching the Tools to the Task: Designing a Publishing System

The right-aligned or decimal tab ensures that numbers will be properly aligned.

Unnumbered Lists

Unnumbered and unbulleted lists are often instructional information that is not step-by-step in nature. Such lists should be indented from both margins and set in a smaller point size or with tighter leading.

Summary

In this chapter, you learned how to affect the readability of your documents by paying attention to the type itself, margins and columns, justification methods and the color of type. You also learned to use special characters, when they are indicated. You gained an understanding of combining rules with type to enhance readability, and to call attention to specific elements or details. In addition, you learned how to produce various types of lists that enhance the usefulness of documents.

88

CHAPTER 5

Controlling Type within Documents

As you have seen in the previous chapters, type needs to be controlled in order to be used well. You're probably familiar with making manual adjustments in type — setting font, size, alignment and, perhaps, even kerning and tracking. While tweaking a document manually is almost always necessary, your word-processing or page-layout program has many controls that will take care of most of your type control issues automatically.

In this chapter we'll deal with setting automation features. We will then tackle knowing when and how to override them with human controls. As we mentioned in Chapter 4, we will reference features and menus from a variety of programs. Your program may use different terms or have other features. You may also find that your program does not have some of the features mentioned. Most higher-end composition programs will have the ability to perform these functions somewhere within the program.

Styled Type vs. Type Styles

There is always discussion — in the Macintosh community — about the difference between using styled type and selecting the "actual" type style from the font menu. This is not an issue when working under Windows because using styled type is the only way to choose italic, bold or bold italic.

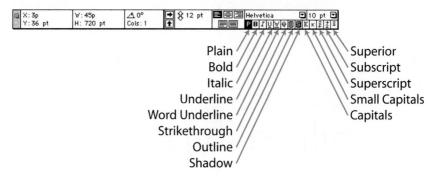

	Plain	Superior
Bold		Subscript
Italic		Superscript
Underline		Small Capitals
Word Underline		Capitals
Strikethrough
Outline
Shadow

The Measurements Palette in QuarkXPress is representative of the font-selection mechanism of most publishing programs.

In the early days of the Macintosh, when a user clicked on the Bold or Italic icons instead of selecting from the font menu, the font was artificially embolded or obliqued. As font-management programs were introduced this problem was resolved. If the user clicked on bold or italic, the bold or italic font was accessed.

What happens when there is no bold or italic for the font? Programs — and programming in the fonts themselves — treat the issue differently. In almost every case the image on the monitor will become bold or italic. If there is no bold for the font, however, the document will print in the base font (Clarendon Light will print as Clarendon Light since there is no bold assigned to it.) Some fonts will print an oblique when the italic does not exist, and some will print the italic as roman, depending upon how the font is programmed to handle that issue.

Compounding the issue are fonts that have more than simply a roman and a bold version of the font. Let's see how complex this issue can become:

Font	Bold	Font	Bold
Garamond Light	**Bold**	Garamond Light Cond.	
Garamond Book		Garamond Book Cond.	**Bold**
Garamond Bold		**Garamond Bold Cond.**	
Garamond Ultra		**Garamond Ultra Cond.**	

When ITC Garamond Light is in use and bold is selected from the palette, the result is Garamond Bold; no other ITC Garamond weight has a paired bold. When using ITC Garamond Condensed, however, the Book weight is paired with bold; no other ITC Garamond Condensed weight has a paired bold.

Other typefaces have similar problems. For example, Adobe Minion Regular is paired with Semibold, not Bold, as you might expect when selecting bold. The Helvetica Neu family is completely unpaired. Because of the dissimilarities between type families, it is best to select typefaces from the menu rather than clicking on bold or pressing Command-B or Control-B.

The other elements found in type-styling menus also bear discussion. Underline, Word Underline, Strikethrough, Outline and Shadow should be used only if there is a compelling reason. For example, the underline style could be used when imitating a hyperlink.

> *Underlines have been used as a substitute for italics when italic fonts were not available. They have also been used in copy markup to indicate that the typesetter is to use italics. With italic fonts available, underlines are, for the most part, unnecessary.*

The choices on the right side of the palette — capitals, small caps, superscript, subscript and superior — can be used with few repercussions. There are some programs, however, when capitals and small capitals are selected from the menu, that create PDF files incorrectly. Also if the typeface has real small caps (selected from an expert font set), those characters should be used in preference to the created small caps.

Hyphenation and Justification

This function, also known as "H&J," is one of the most important and least understood of the functions involved in the composition process. When your system is set up well, it relieves you of the tedium of constantly intervening with the type you set.

Hyphenation and justification are two interactive functions. Hyphenation can be set (program-dependent) to control:

- the minimum number of characters a word must contain before hyphenation is allowed

- the minimum number of characters that must occur before the hyphen

- the minimum number of characters that must occur after a hyphenation point

- the maximum number of hyphens allowed in a row and the zone in which hyphenation is allowed, called the "hyphenation zone"

In this hyphenation zone, the hyphenation function examines a word to determine whether or not it contains a hyphenatable point and so should be hyphenated and wrapped to the next line. If a space occurs within the zone, no hyphenation occurs. If there is no hyphenatable point in a word within the zone, the entire word breaks to the next line.

> Wild and crazy type can be a very good thing, if the circumstances for introducing it are right. ◉ Type doesn't have to be *boring* in order to reside in a document people can read. ⌛ In fact, this entire section, complete with dingbats, is comprised of type.

Type to the right of the dashed line is in the hyphenation zone.

When setting up hyphenation routines — especially when defining a hyphenation zone — you must take into account the nature of the document, house standards and the line length with which you are working. If you are creating a marketing piece, you will want to eliminate hyphenation entirely, if possible. A newsletter with narrower columns usually requires more hyphenation than a book. Setting the hyphenation zone also helps control the raggedness of flush-left text.

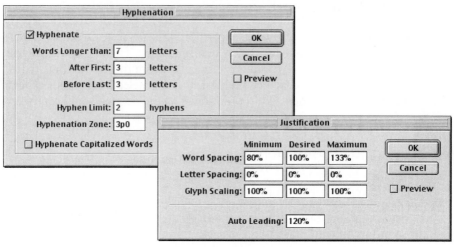

The Hyphenation and Justification menus from Adobe InDesign are accessed separately.

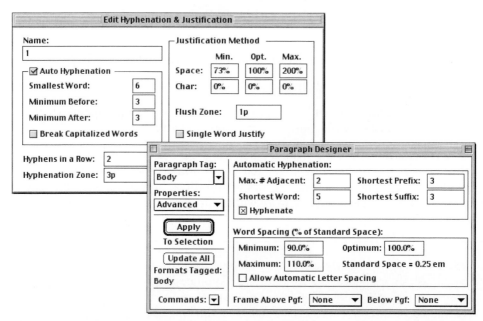

Both QuarkXPress (upper left) and Adobe FrameMaker (lower right) combine the Hyphenation and Justification menus since the functions interact.

Justification is controlled through adjusting word spacing, letter spacing and in the case of Adobe InDesign, glyph scaling. When your program justifies lines, it first tries to do so using the parameters for word space. It then includes allowed parameters for character space. As a last resort, it hyphenates the line.

Most programs hyphenate on a line-by-line basis. As a result, one line may be relatively tightly spaced while the next line may be loosely spaced. Some software has an optional multiline composition option, which uses a preset number of lines to make its hyphenation decisions. This usually results in better overall composition of long documents.

Auto vs. Manual Hyphenation

It is much faster to use a program's automatic hyphenation routine than to hyphenate manually. When you take the time to set it up properly, you achieve excellent results with very little manual interaction. Some programs, such as QuarkXPress, require that you preset hyphenation and justification routines and apply the presets to individual paragraphs or styles. Other programs, such as Adobe InDesign, require you to set hyphenation and justification in each paragraph or style; the last hyphenation setting created acts as the default.

There are advantages to both methods. Working with presets, when properly constructed, gives the compositor greater latitude. For example, text presets may allow hyphenation, and degrees of looseness or tightness. A preset that does not allow hyphenation could be used for callouts or headlines.

When working on advertising typography — particularly when composing short documents like ads — the number-of-hyphens-in-a-row setting should be set to one, or hyphenation should be turned off. Multiline composition options should not be used when setting advertising typography.

Some tricks to forcing good H&J were hinted at in Chapter 4. A problem you especially want to avoid is that of inserting a hyphen manually and then having the lines rewrap when edits are made. You can't control the rewrapping of lines, but you can ensure that you won't have a hyphen in the middle of a line.

When you need to break a word manually or force a word not to hyphenate at all, you should use a discretionary hyphen. When a *discretionary hyphen* is used instead of a standard hyphen, the hyphen will only be inserted if the word must break to a second line. A discretionary hyphen placed in front of a word will cause that word to remain as a unit, unhyphenated.

If there are words that you never want to hyphenate, they can be placed in an auxiliary or user's dictionary. An *auxiliary dictionary* is one to which you add specific words and indicate what hyphenation is allowed. If you allow no hyphenation points, the word will never automatically hyphenate.

	Nonbreaking Space	Discretionary Hyphen	Nonbreaking Hyphen
Macintosh			
Adobe FrameMaker	Opt-[Space]	Cmd--[Hyphen]	Esc--[Hyphen]-h
Adobe InDesign	Opt-[Space]	Cmd-Shift--[Hyphen]	Cmd-Opt--[Hyphen]
Adobe PageMaker	Opt-[Space]	Cmd-Shift--[Hyphen]	Cmd-Opt--[Hyphen]
QuarkXPress	Cmd-[Space]	Cmd--[Hyphen]	
Windows			
Adobe FrameMaker	Ctrl-[Space]	Ctrl--[Hyphen]	Esc--[Hyphen-h]
Adobe InDesign	Ctrl-Alt-x	Ctrl-Shift--[Hyphen]	Ctrl-Alt--[Hyphen]
Adobe PageMaker	Ctrl-Alt-[Space]	Ctrl-Shift--[Hyphen]	Ctrl-Alt--[Hyphen]
QuarkXPress	Ctrl-[Space]	Ctrl--[Hyphen]	

Four much-used publishing programs access nonbreaking characters differently.

When you want two separate words to stay together, such as "St. Petersburg," you can use a nonbreaking space. A nonbreaking space, unlike a fixed space, will change its width in justified text but will not allow a line break.

412. **Kickapoo Indian Sagwa Paper sign,** copyright 1892. One of the finest if not the The Finest paper sign known. 28"×42" – color is perfect. J. Ohman Litho. Wonderful oak frame. (25,000–35,000)
Insert non-breaking space here.

413. 43½"×27½" **paper printers proof** (Forbes Litho) **Everett Piano.** Has been torn in half and repaired. Great Boston scene. (1,500–1,800)
Insert discretionary hyphen here to prevent hyphenation.

414. **Outrageous Coca Cola sign.** Hand painted lady's face with actual scarf tie, 21 tall. Has hanger on the back. Minor edge damage. Crazing to lady's face. A very unusual piece. Also a bend in the cardboard on the left hand side. (300–500)

This selection, taken from an auction catalog, shows where nonbreaking spaces and discretionary hyphens can be added to ensure that the document will not change if edits are made to the text.

Fixed spaces, or tabbed text with hanging indents, should be used for numbered or bulleted lists when the text is justified. This will cause the left margin of the text to remain constant.

- Design experience from 1 watt to the kilowatt range

- Fully staffed prototype lab

- Rapid prototype development and delivery — usually within one week or less

- Pre-production run components — from 25–50 pieces

- Engineering lab utilizes production techniques to ensure manufacturability in volume production

- Samples supplied with full test data

In this example, we incorrectly used normal justifying spaces after the bullets instead of fixed spaces or tabs. Note how irregular the left margin is when lines are allowed to justify.

Reworking "Rivers" of Type in a Column

An added reason for choosing an appropriate line length when working with type justified to both margins is the phenomenon known as "rivers". A *river* — wide running areas of white space between words — occurs when the hyphenation and justification routines are set improperly, or when the column is too narrow for the point size used. We often see this in newspaper text.

At this the whole pack rose up into the air, and came flying down upon her: she gave a little scream, half of fright and half of anger, and tried to beat them off, and found herself lying on the bank, with her head in the lap of her sister, who was gently brushing away some dead leaves that had fluttered down from the trees upon her face.

Rivers can be managed, for the most part, by choosing a line length that is appropriate to the type face and size, and by properly setting H&Js. Sometimes they must be overridden manually, employing your skills of kerning and tracking. In a worst-case scenario, the document must be redesigned.

Note the wide areas of space running through this sample of text.

Horizontal and Vertical Alignment

There are a variety of tools available for aligning type both horizontally and vertically. After H&J parameters are set, indents — whether for the entire paragraph or just for the first line — should be managed through the paragraph menu. This is also true for space above or below paragraphs. You should never add interparagraph space by double-spacing.

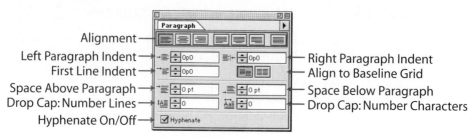

Alignment
Left Paragraph Indent
First Line Indent
Space Above Paragraph
Drop Cap: Number Lines
Hyphenate On/Off

Right Paragraph Indent
Align to Baseline Grid
Space Below Paragraph
Drop Cap: Number Characters

This graphic shows an example of the options available through paragraph menus. This menu is from Adobe InDesign and shows the basic paragraph-spacing commands.

Aligning pages vertically is an art. Often the designer will want the lines of text to align on a multicolumn page. This would seem to be a simple task. Headlines are larger than body text, however, and require different leading. When this is desired, careful attention must be paid to both the design and composition stages to force alignment.

ATTRACTIONS

The Children's Museum 603/555-3853. 280 Marcy St., Portsmouth. T-Sat 10–5 pm, Sun 1–5 pm. Hands-on exhibits for children.

Fuller Gardens 603/555-5414. 10 Willow Ave. North Hampton. Mid May–Oct Daily 10 am–6 pm. Two acres of formal gardens, featuring roses, perennials, annuals, a Japanese garden and a conservatry. An All-American Rose Display Garden.

Hampton Beach Casino "The Family Fun Center" 603/555-4541. Ocean Blvd, Hampton Beach. Seven acres of fun for the whole family. Gift shops, restaurants, arcades, mini-golf, fast food, kiddies rides, waterslides and much, much more.

Hilltop Fun Center 603/555-8068. Rte 108, Somersworth. The largest family amusement center in the Seacoast area. Miniature golf, go-karts, batting cages, driving range, bumper boats and arcade. Open daily April–October.

Portsmouth Harbor Cruises (800) 555-0915 or (603) 555-8084. 64 Ceres St., Portsmouth. Explore Portsmouth Harbor, Inland Rivers, Sunset, Foliage Cruises. Private charters on the 49-passenger *M/V Heritage.* Full bar and galley. Sail charters on 40' ketch *Irie.*

The Raspberry Farm 603/555-6604. Rte 86, Hampton Falls. Scenic colonial NH farm with fresh raspberries, blackberries and strawberries, to pick or buy from June–Oct. Homemade Raspberry Sauce, Jams and freshly baked Raspberry Pie.

Seacoast Greyhound Park 603/555-3065. Rte 107, Seabrook. Climate controlled, with fine dining, restaurant, lounge, snack bars, and function room. Year round fun, and now simulcasting horseracing, too. Matinee and evening performances.

Water Country 603/555-3556. Rte 1, Portsmouth. New England's largest water park. Polaroid Shoot, The Screamer, Huge Wave Pool, Adventure River, Giant Waterslides, Whirlpool, Octopus Lagoon — great family fun. Spend the day!

Note the problems with vertical alignment in this selection. The leading is 9 pt., with an additional 3 pt. before each paragraph. The first headline is in a larger point size so it drops lower on the page than the text in the second column. How would you fix the vertical justification?

In the preceding example, 12 pt. additional space would have to be inserted between "Attractions" and the first line of text to make the lines justify line for line and justify equally at the bottom of the page. This is because all paragraphs have an equal number of lines except for the first one. If any intervening paragraph had a different number of lines, the task could be impossible.

How would you change the text block? Would you align the lines across, align the bottoms, leave it as it is, rework the columns or change the interparagraph leading? There are many options.

Vertical justification — the process of aligning text so that tops and bottoms are equal — is undertaken by adding space in two different ways or by using both methods together. *Carding* involves adding equal amounts of space between each paragraph, as required by the individual column. *Feathering* adds equal amounts of space between each line in each column. The two methods can be used in combination.

ATTRACTIONS

The Children's Museum 603/555-3853 280 Marcy St., Portsmouth. T-Sat 10–5 pm, Sun 1–5 pm. Hands-on exhibits for children.

Fuller Gardens 603/555-5414 10 Willow Ave. North Hampton. Mid May–Oct Daily 10 am–6 pm. Two acres of formal gardens, featuring roses, perennials, annuals, a Japanese garden and a conservatry. An All-American Rose Display Garden.

Hampton Beach Casino "The Family Fun Center" 603/555-4541 Ocean Blvd, Hampton Beach. Seven acres of fun for the whole family. Gift shops, restaurants, arcades, mini-golf, fast food, kiddies rides, waterslides and much, much more.

Hilltop Fun Center 603/555-8068 Rte 108, Somersworth. The largest family amusement center in the Seacoast area. Miniature golf, go-karts, batting cages, driving range, bumper boats and arcade. Open daily April–October.

Portsmouth Harbor Cruises (800) 555-0915 or (603) 555-8084. 64 Ceres St., Portsmouth. Explore Portsmouth Harbor, Inland Rivers, Sunset, Foliage Cruises. Private charters on the 49-passenger *M/V Heritage*. Full bar and galley. Sail charters on 40′ ketch *Irie*.

The Raspberry Farm 603/555-6604 Rte. 86, Hampton Falls. Scenic colonial NH farm with fresh raspberries, blackberries and strawberries, to pick or buy from June–Oct. Homemade Raspberry Sauce, James and freshly baked Raspberry Pie.

Seacoast Greyhound Park 603/555-3065 Rte 107, Seabrook. Climate controlled, with fine dining, restaurant, lounge, snack bars, and function room. Year round fun, and now simulcasting horseracing, too. Matinee and evening performances.

Water Country 603/555-3556 Rte. 1, Portsmouth. New England's largest water park. Polaroid Shoot, The Screamer, Huge Wave Pool, Adventure River, Giant Waterslides, Whirlpool, Octopus Lagoon — great family fun. Spend the day!

In this example, we carded the paragraphs, inserting the rule between the columns so the eye would be less confused by the different positions of the lines.

Interparagraph spacing can lead to reading difficulties since all text may not line up horizontally. It is often better, in long running text with multiple columns, to use paragraph indents instead of space above or below paragraphs. When designing space for headlines, the total space (space above, space below and leading) should be a multiple of the leading of the body text. Even when such planning is put into effect, a heading that lands at the top of a column may throw the leading off. A heading that is two lines instead of one may also cause manual intervention.

Another solution that almost all programs allow is the ability to lock paragraphs to a publication grid, which can be based on the leading or on any increment you like.

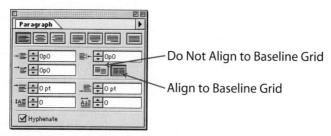

—Do Not Align to Baseline Grid

—Align to Baseline Grid

The Paragraph palette for Adobe InDesign allows you to align any paragraph to the baseline grid.

The grid can be started at any point on the page, with individual paragraphs aligning — or not — at the designer's option.

Grid starts 36 pt down from zero. →

Grid increment → is every 12 pt.

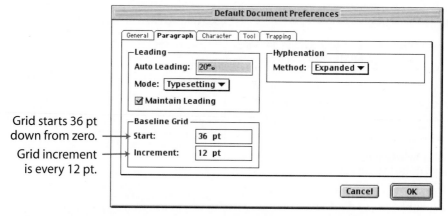

In QuarkXPress the baseline grid design is part of Document Preferences. It can be started at any position from the zero point, and increments are set to the designer's specifications. The document grid may be turned on or off for any paragraph and applies to all pages in the document.

While this seems like an easy solution to aligning lines across columns, it often presents unanticipated design problems. When a grid is used, all paragraphs set to align to the grid will do so, regardless of their specified leading or spacing above or below.

In this example, the baseline grid begins 14 pt. from the border of the page and advances in increments of 3 pt. Type is set 8/9 with an additional 3 pt. above each paragraph. What would happen if the type were aligned to a grid with 9 pt. increments?

Because of the side effects of vertically justifying text, it has become a standard practice, in many types of publications (including this book), to leave the bottom margins irregular. When designing publications it is essential that you take into account the variables and specify where liberties may be taken.

Widow & Orphan Control

Widows and orphans are often misunderstood. A *widow* occurs when the last line of a paragraph is forced to the next column or page. An *orphan* occurs when the first line of a paragraph falls at the bottom of a column or page. Widows and orphans are undesirable because they hinder the readability of the document and are unattractive.

Four score and seven years ago our fathers brought forth, upon this continent, a new nation, conceived in Liberty, and dedicated to the proposition that all men are created equal.

Now we are engaged in a great civil war, testing whether that nation, or any nation so conceived, and so dedicated, can long endure. We are met here on a great battlefield of that war. We have come to dedicate a portion of it as a final resting place for those who here gave their lives that that nation might live. It is altogether fitting and proper that we should do this.

But in a larger sense we can not dedicate – we can not consecrate – we can not hallow this ground. The brave men, living and dead, who struggled, here, have consecrated it far above our poor power to add or detract.

The world will little note, nor long remember, what we say here, but can never forget what they did here. It is for us, the living, rather to be dedicated here to the unfinished work which they have, thus far, so nobly carried on. It is rather for us to be here dedicated to the great task remaining before us – that from these honored dead we take increased devotion to that cause for which they here gave the last full measure of devotion – that we here highly resolve that these dead shall not have died in vain; that this nation shall have a new birth of freedom; and that this government of the people, by the people, for the people, shall not perish from the earth.

Four score and seven years ago our fathers brought forth, upon this continent, a new nation, conceived in Liberty, and dedicated to the proposition that all men are created equal.

Now we are engaged in a great civil war, testing whether that nation, or any nation so conceived, and so dedicated, can long endure. We are met here on a great battlefield of that war. We have come to dedicate a portion of it as a final resting place for those who here gave their lives that that nation might live. It is altogether fitting and proper that we should do this.

But in a larger sense we can not dedicate – we can not consecrate – we can not hallow this ground. The brave men, living and dead, who struggled, here, have consecrated it far above our poor power to add or detract.

The world will little note, nor long remember, what we say here, but can never forget what they did here. It is for us, the living, rather to be dedicated here to the unfinished work which they have, thus far, so nobly carried on. It is rather for us to be here dedicated to the great task remaining before us – that from these honored dead we take increased devotion to that cause for which they here gave the last full measure of devotion – that we here highly resolve that these dead shall not have died in vain; that this nation shall have a new birth of freedom; and that this government of the people, by the people, for the people, shall not perish from the earth.

Widow (left) and orphan (right). Widows are thrust ahead while orphans are left behind.

Widows and orphans are controlled through the Keep section of paragraph menus.

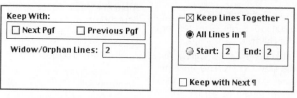

Keep dialog boxes from Adobe FrameMaker (left) and QuarkXPress (right).

Many are familiar with still another type of widow, the short last line of a paragraph. We call these "word widows" to distinguish them from paragraph widows. Paragraph three of the preceding illustration has such a widow.

Every publishing group has its own house style specifying what constitutes a word widow. Some define it by the percentage of the line it occupies, others by the number of characters. There is general agreement that a single short word or a part of a word that has been hyphenated from the preceding line are widows and should be avoided. Unfortunately this capability is not built into composition programs. Lines must be proofread and reworked manually to either add words to the line or work the text up into the previous line.

Working with Styles

Styles are, without question, the most powerful means at your disposal to ensure consistency within your documents and to automatically apply multiple attributes to characters and to paragraphs. For example, the color, style, leading and even H&J values can be included in a style and applied to a paragraph with a single mouse click. Styles can even be applied in a word-processing program; they are applied automatically to the paragraphs when the text is imported.

To make styles most useful, you should always use the same designations for styles. You are not taking full advantage of the consistency that you can achieve through the use of styles if you use T, H1, H2 and BL for text, first and second level headlines, and bulleted lists in one document, then use Text, Heading 1, Heading 2 and Bullet in another document.

It is the responsibility of the editorial group to assign hierarchical levels to the document and to ensure that the hierarchy is maintained. It is the design group's responsibility to assign the appearance of each style. For example, the T style (body text) could be Minion 11/13 in one publication and Sabon 10/11 in another.

@H1:Summary
@T1:Preparing electronic manuscripts is very
important to the publishing process. When
the job is done correctly, everyone
benefits. The work is financially rewarding
for the text entry person; the job flows
through composition smoothly; the publisher
can expect to receive the final product in
a timely manner with few (if any) errors.
@T:It is very important, therefore, to be
sure you understand all the directions
before you begin. The old carpenter's maxim
<I>measure ten times, cut once<$> come into
play when you prepare electronic
manuscripts. Of course, if you have
questions about the manuscript, you should
call your contact person.
@BL1:Read all your directions carefully and
be sure you understand them before you
begin.
@BL:Use the coding instructions you have
been provided. Do not make up codes as you
go along.
@BL:Type styles exactly as they are written
(if the style is <I>H1<$>, don't type
<I>H-1<$>). if a style seems to be
inconsistent, call your contact person for
clarification.
@BL2:If you have questions, <I>ask<$>. Never
assume.
@T:We look forward to enjoying a long and
mutually rewarding relationship together.

Summary

Preparing electronic manuscripts is very important to the publishing process. When the job is done correctly, everyone benefits. The work is financially rewarding for the text entry person; the job flows through composition smoothly; the publisher can expect to receive the final product in a timely manner with few (if any) errors.

It is very important, therefore, to be sure you understand all the directions before you begin. The old carpenter's maxim *measure ten times, cut once* come into play when you prepare electronic manuscripts. Of course, if you have questions about the manuscript, you should call your contact person.

- Read all your directions carefully and be sure you understand them before you begin.
- Use the coding instructions you have been provided. Do not make up codes as you go along.
- Type styles exactly as they are written (if the style is *H1*, don't type *H-1*). if a style seems to be inconsistent, call your contact person for clarification.
- If you have questions, *ask*. Never assume.

We look forward to enjoying a long and mutually rewarding relationship together.

In this sample of electronically marked-up text, the styles are shown in blue. The translation of style names to the styled document is at the right. Six styles were used, three of them bullet styles, to insert different amounts of space above, within and below the bulleted list.

Interaction of Styles

Well-developed styles can do more than just affect the appearance of the type. They can be used for widow and orphan control, and to keep elements together on the page.

Paragraph Attributes

Formats | Tabs | Rules

Left Indent: 0p
First Line: 0p
Right Indent: 0p

☐ Drop Caps
Character Count: 1
Line Count: 3

Leading: 18 pt ▼
Space Before: 10 pt
Space After: 8 pt

☒ Keep Lines Together
● All Lines in ¶
○ Start: 2 End: 2

Alignment: Left ▼
H&J: None ▼

☒ Keep with Next ¶
☐ Lock to Baseline Grid

[Apply] [Cancel] [OK]

Here the paragraph attributes for a headline style clearly show interaction with other paragraphs. Spacing above and below is automatic — all lines in the paragraph will be kept together, and the headline will stay with the following paragraph.

As we noticed in the preceding illustration, we can use styles to force paragraphs to stay together — the entire paragraph will remain in a single column or on a single page. This is particularly useful when working with headlines and bulleted lists. The headline can be forced to remain intact, moving to the next page or the next column in preference to breaking the headline in two parts. It can also be forced to continue with the following paragraph, assuring that a headline will never end up at the bottom of a page.

When preparing your documents, be sure to work out clearly the style sheet for the entire document and to test each style and all possible style interactions. For example, some book formats allow one headline to follow another immediately, with no intervening text. As a result, we could have a collection of headline styles that reflects the interaction of styles.

Headline Styles

H1	Level 1	Myriad Bold, 18/20, blue, sentence case, align left, 15 pt. before, 5 pt. after, keep all lines together, keep with next paragraph, hyphenation off
H2	Level 2	Same as H1, except 14/16, 12 pt. before, 4 pt. after
H2-1	2 following 1	Same as H2, except no space before
H3	Level 2	Same as H1, except 12/14, 11.5 pt. before, 2.5 pt. after
H3-2	3 following 2	Same as H3, except no space before
H4	Level 4	Sabon Bold, 11/13, sentence case, align justified, period and em space after headline and run in with text, hyphenation on

Sometimes it is necessary to create multiple styles for the same type of headline to allow for interaction with other type styles.

If you take the time to build a good *style sheet* (the combination of all styles used in the document), you will find that creating documents — from ads to annual reports — is accomplished more quickly and with fewer errors than if you style each element manually. If your styles are always named similarly, you will even further automate your production.

Summary

We have seen in this chapter how working with the underpinnings of documents — H&Js, alignment and vertical justification, widow and orphan control, and styles — helps us build consistent documents that flow together. By using the tools of our trade, we are able to speed production and enhance documents. We do this by paying attention to details, such as eliminating rivers, while fine-tuning justification and ragged text.

SECTION 3

REAL-WORLD CHALLENGES

*Printing should be invisible. Type well-used is invisible as type.
The mental eye focuses through type and not upon it, so that any
type which has excess in design, anything that gets in the way of
the mental picture to be conveyed, is bad type.*

— BEATRICE WARD

Whether designing for print or electronic distribution, or managing fonts in the a printing environment, we follow principles that have been set in place by others. Some of these are principles of design; others are limitations imposed by the medium or by the processes we're required to use. It's been argued that the difference between plagiarism and a creative idea is a designer's ability to forget where he or she first saw the idea. Daniel Webster commented, "I see nothing in [design] that's new and valuable. What is valuable is not new, and what is new is not valuable."

In this section, we try to avoid setting hard-and-fast rules, choosing instead to present as many design options as possible. The best designers are those that are able to meet assignments with a "what-if" approach. While experimentation isn't likely to uncover bold new paths, it will give you and your client options, and you will become a better designer than if you stick to only what you already know.

Matching type to the message is an important function of design. Sometimes it involves invoking the typeface's personality, and at other times it is simply a matter of using good sense. For years, printers have stipulated, "when in doubt, use Baskerville" because the typeface is strong but doesn't overshadow the message. Some typefaces are better suited for lengthy text; others are more appropriate for shorter copy elements and headlines. When working with less text-intensive documents it is easier to be creative in the selection of type. Just remember that type should never confuse or obscure the message.

Although there are thousands of faces available, avoid mixing too many families on a page. It's important that your type appear "comfortable" on the page — with neither neither too much nor too little space around it.

Type objects that serve a graphic function — like headlines, banners, buttons and the like, should be subject to the same considerations as any other graphic object. These include color, contrast, transparency, positioning and size. These issues come into even greater play when developing a logo using type (something often referred to as "logo-type").

Of course, challenges in print are only part of the story today. Web designers face a number of different challenges. They must make pages interesting but still allow them to load rapidly. They can't be sure that the fonts they use for text blocks will be available on the viewer's system (although they can make graphical type elements for display purposes). They don't have nearly the room to tell a story on a monitor that they do on paper. These are only a few of the differences between type for print and type for Web or interactive display.

Adding to the confusion about Web type is the fact that some processes that work with today's edition of HTML will not work with future versions. Instead, solutions such as Cascading Style Sheets (CSS) will be employed. CSS promises to someday allow designers to embed fonts in documents in a way that protects the font creator's intellectual property rights.

No book about type would be complete without a discussion of font technologies. From the three most common font technologies — PostScript, TrueType and Open Type — to the internal workings of fonts, we help you understand fonts from a technical and mechanical standpoint. You will explore the technique of font matching and discover why it sometimes fails. Managing fonts on your computer can be a big undertaking, especially if you've installed hundreds — even thousands — of faces. Coming up with an effective filing system can be a chore. You'll explore several ways to accomplish this logistical task.

Managing fonts in a printing workflow and troubleshooting associated problems is another area we'll discuss. You'll learn how to avoid problems and how to troubleshoot common PostScript errors.

When you complete this section, you will be familiar with many of the typographic challenges facing graphic artists today, and be prepared to meet them head on.

CHAPTER 6

Designing with Type

What most of us enjoy about type is putting it to work on the page. Whether we're working with headlines or other applications of display type, or with a substantial amount of body text, getting just the right look is often a challenge. So far, you have examined the primary type categories, explored how to make type more readable and learned a number of dos and don'ts about working with type.

In the process we have, we hope, dispelled some myths about type — such as the idea that serif fonts are easier to read than sans-serif fonts or that type set in all caps is easy to read at all. You have also learned about the color of type and have explored some features of character sets other than the standard sets. For the most part our discussion to date has been technical.

In this chapter, we'll apply much of what we have learned to the actual use of type on the page. As noted before, you should be able to perform any of these functions with a capable page-layout program or illustration program. Design-intensive functions cannot be easily accomplished, usually, using a word-processing program.

Matching Type to the Message

When speaking with designers or typographers, you will often hear them speak of the "feel" of a given typeface. Not surprisingly, type does have a personality. Sometimes the personality of the type is subjective. For example, several years ago ITC Souvenir and ITC Korinna were overused. Everywhere you looked you saw these distinctive typefaces. Some designers (and many typographers) banned the typefaces from their studios 'til this very day.

| It matters not how beautiful a type-face may be if it is overused, or simply used improperly. The type-face will gain a bad reputation and designers will spurn its glyphs. | It matters not how beautiful a typeface may be if it is over-used, or simply used improperly. The typeface will gain a bad rep-utation and designers will spurn its glyphs. |

In the 1970s and 1980s, ITC Souvenir (left) and ITC Korinna (right) were overused. Originally designed as headline faces, they found their way into far too much body text.

Some typefaces have their personality designed into them, or have become accepted for specific uses over the years. "When in doubt," say old-time printers, "use Baskerville." Others have their primary use included in their name, such as Century Schoolbook.

Type Denotation and Connotation

Denotation is the direct meaning or set of meaning of a word or expression — it is also the specific use for which the typeface was designed. *Connotation* is the set of ideas or meanings associated with a word or suggested by it — it is also the feelings that we associate with a particular typeface because of our experience and because of customary usage.

Using common sense will often help in our typeface selection. For example, using Comic Sans or a Grunge face would be inappropriate for a funeral home — unless you have a very strange sense of humor.

To an Australian, a bonzer is an object or action so well constructed, or so accomplished that it fits its use to perfection. The word was introduced to Americans during World War II.

To an Australian, a bonzer is an object or action so well constructed, or so accomplished that it fits its use to perfection. The word was introduced to Americans during World War II.

To an Australian, a bonzer is an object or action so well constructed, or so accomplished that it fits its use to perfection. The word was introduced to Americans during World War II.

All three of these typefaces are designed as book faces. From top to bottom, they are New Century Schoolbook, Linotype Design Staff, 1980, based on Morris Fuller Benton's 1919 design; ITC Garamond Book, Tony Stan, 1975; and Bodoni Book, Morris Fuller Benton, 1910, based on Giambattista Bodoni's 1798 designs.

Other typefaces were named to describe the typeface, rather than its function.

If you've been taken to the cleaners, chances are you won't be steppin' out in style, since you have just lost your money through gambling, or having been robbed or cheated.

Organon is anything that serves as an instrument to facilitate the acquisition of knowledge (such as reading these little type blurbs).

PEOPLE HAVE BEEN SUBJECT TO OFF-BEAT BEHAVIOR SINCE THE DAWN OF TIME, BUT ONLY SINCE 1935 HAS THAT WHICH IS WEIRD, UNCONVENTIONAL (BUT NOT UNIQUE) HAD A SPECIFIC NAME.

These typefaces were named to describe their function. ITC Clearface, Victor Caruso, 1978, based on Morris Fuller Benton's 1908 design (top) and Optima, Hermann Zapf, 1958 (middle), are both clean, easy-to-read fonts. Orator, originally used on the IBM Selectric typewriter, was intended to be an easy-to-read font for speakers reading their notes as they gave speeches.

Aside from the word "script," included as part of the name, a number of Script faces describe more clearly the nature or use of the typeface.

Metonymy is a rhetorical device in which an attribute or related concept is substituted for the name of another.

If you're headed for nowheresville, you're headed for a jerkwater town, suitable only for those who are square, dull, and corny.

An eggbeater is a woman's hairstyle, shoulder length or shorter, featuring a tousled, windblown, almost disheveled look.

The names of these Scripts indicate their look or their use. They are, from top to bottom: Brush Script, Robert E. Smith, 1942; Nuptial Script, Edwin Shaar, 1952; Poetica Chancery III, Robert Slimbach, 1998.

An apple polisher is one who curries favor from a superior, specifically a student who gives his teacher a bribe and expects good grades.

Getting the axe is a sudden separation from one's job, a quick dismissal from school or a terminal rejection from one's lover or spouse.

ants in the pants is an inability to sit still, to fidget with anxiety, lust, or eagerness.

As is true of the typefaces above, the names often indicate the nature of the face. From top to bottom, they are ITC American Typewriter, Jack Kadan and Tony Stan, 1974; Comic Sans, Vincent Connare, 1995; and American Uncial, Victor Hammer, 1953.

In addition to fonts used for text, many Pi fonts have names that clearly describe the nature of the type, while other names are somewhat less explicit. For example, Wingdings, Thingbats and Patterns One and Two give little information, while Carta, Monotype Botanical and Linotype Game Pi tell us what to expect to find in the font.

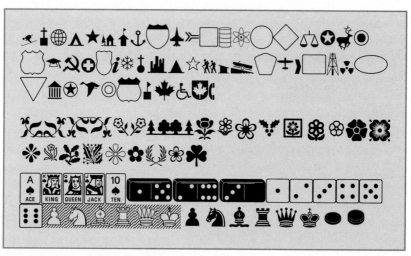

The names of these Pi fonts give us a good indication of what we'll find in the font. They are (top to bottom) Carta, Lynne Garrell, 1986; Monotype Botanical Pi and Linotype Game Pi.

Other fonts, while not having descriptive names, suggest their intended use by their very design. While many typefaces can be used as general-purpose type, some are ideally suited to given applications. One such example is the many flowing scripts, which often appear on wedding announcements, invitations and sympathy cards.

> *Have you heard of a kakistocracy?*
> *It's a government run by*
> *the worst people in the state.*
>
> *Think you have poise? It was originally a unit used in measuring*
> *viscosity. The adaptation is that a poised person has sufficient self*
> *esteem to go with the flow of public opinion.*
>
> *Coined by Horace Walpole in 1754,*
> *after the three princes of Serendip, who*
> *in their travels always gained by*
> *chance things they did not seek, our*
> *language has embrace serendipity.*

These flowing scripts all have multiple weights and a distinctive appearance. All are set in 18 pt., but vary considerably in the size of the actual letters. These faces are (top to bottom) Künstler Medium, Hans Bohn, 1957; Palace Script Semibold, Monotype Design Studio, 1923; and Snell Roundhand Bold, Matthew Carter, 1972.

Some fonts were designed for specific uses, such as the Orator font we discussed earlier in this chapter.

> Leaking official or secret information can have a multitude of results; misinformation can be disseminated without it ever coming back to haunt the leak(er); governments have been using this trick for years.
>
> Anyone or anything that is an outstanding example, of extraordiary size, appearance, quality, force or absurdity can be described as a lulu. The term is used both derisively and admiringly.

Lucida and Lucida Sans, designed by Charles Bigelow and Kris Holmes in 1985, are ideal fonts for faxing. They hold up especially well with the dot-matrix print customarily in use at that time.

When attempting to set large amounts of text within a confined space, you will need to use fonts with a high count of characters per inch. You should also avoid condensed typefaces which are, by their nature, harder to read. Note the differences in the readability of the typefaces below and the amount of type that will fit the space.

> Its Latin derivation is the source of either one hundred dollars or a hundred dollar bill being called a century. No matter what the denomination, currency is appreciated.
>
> Its Latin derivation is the source of either one hundred dollars or a hundred dollar bill being called a century. No matter what the denomination, currency is appreciated.
>
> Its Latin derivation is the source of either one hundred dollars or a hundred dollar bill being called a century. No matter what the denomination, currency is appreciated.
>
> Its Latin derivation is the source of either one hundred dollars or a hundred dollar bill being called a century. No matter what the denomination, currency is appreciated.
>
> Its Latin derivation is the source of either one hundred dollars or a hundred dollar bill being called a century. No matter what the denomination, currency is appreciated.

All type in this sampling is set 12/14. The listing of fonts is, from the top down: ITC Century Book and ITC Century Condensed Book, Tony Stan, 1975, 2.11 and 2.51 characters/pica; ITC Cushing Book, Vincent Pacella, 1982, based on designs of J. Stearns and F.W. Goudy, 1897–1904, 2.44 characters/pica; Minion Roman, Robert Slimbach, 1989, 2.47 characters/pica; and Times New Roman, Stanley Morrison, Victor Lardent, Monotype Design Staff, 1931, 2.50 characters/pica.

You can also illustrate a point using type as a graphic. The following examples use this approach to effectively illustrate some common oxymora:

Nadine Fredeling's type samples include candy-like polka dots paired with somberly rendered sorrow, and chilly blue and hot rust pairing to illustrate cold sweat.

Kitsia Padro used color in her typographic allusions, paired with vibrant differences in the texture of the type.

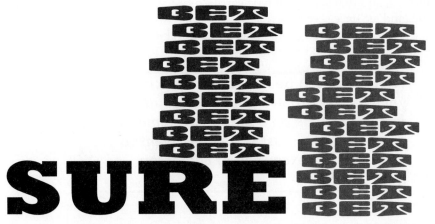

Sarah Lindley's Sure Bet stacks up red and blue chips alongside a solid black "sure"' foundation.

The design or the name of some typefaces suggests specific uses. Most typefaces that spur us to categorize them in this way fall under the category of Display type, which we will discuss next.

Display Type

Display type, also called "headline type," has been used since earliest times. Although decorative alphabets used for passages of text surfaced in the 18th century from English and French foundries, scribes were using illuminated drop caps in the late 7th century. Display type can be outrageous or very straightforward. Its only common feature is that it is designed for use in larger sizes.

This is not to say that everyday typefaces should not be used as display faces. Indeed, the beauty of some typefaces, such as the Bodonis, Avenir and the Garamonds, becomes more striking when they are used in some display settings. While type should match the message, the combination of type styles that you use in each document should also be harmonious.

Using Type for Headlines

When we refer to headlines, we're not talking about titles of magazine articles or type used primarily as a graphic element. Rather, we refer to the larger type that sets apart different sections of an article or a brochure. This type must first of all be easy to read, because it is often the sole element that attracts a readers eye. Cluttering a headline up with froufrou or using bad typographic standards (like using all caps, for the most part) will not draw favorable attention.

So, how do we decide what fonts to use as headlines? First of all, we can look to the body text. Many headlines — especially subheads — can be run in a bolder weight of the body text. It has been suggested that since most body text is a serif face, headlines should be sans serif, and that sans-serif type carries more authority. While this may or may not be true (and we have seen no evidence that it is), two serif faces can peacefully coexist, if they are not so similar in design that they clash. Note the following examples of a variety of mixed and matched headline and text type.

While type can be mixed and matched, you will want to avoid mixing too many families of type on a page. Two families are usually the most you would want to mix, with the exception of characters from a Pi font.

Today, you, too, can look good in print

Not very long ago, preparing good-looking, high-quality documents was a costly and time-consuming process. And on top of all that, companies had minimal control over the documents they produced. It's different today.

This combination of ITC Century Book (Tony Stan, 1975) and Clarendon Bold (Hermann Eidenbenz, 1951) contrasts the two serif styles.

Today, you, too, can look good in print

Not very long ago, preparing good-looking, high-quality documents was a costly and time-consuming process. And on top of all that, companies had minimal control over the documents they produced. It's different today.

Stone Sans Bold (Sumner Stone, 1987) nicely complements the ITC Century Book.

Today, you, too, can look good in print

Not very long ago, preparing good-looking, high-quality documents was a costly and time-consuming process. And on top of all that, companies had minimal control over the documents they produced. It's different today.

Here we have used ITC Goudy Sans Bold (ITC Design Staff, 1986, based on designs by F.W. Goudy, 1929) to pick up the flavor of the Goudy Oldstyle body text while still contrasting with it effectively.

Today, you, too, can look good in print

Not very long ago, preparing good-looking, high-quality documents was a costly and time-consuming process. And on top of all that, companies had minimal control over the documents they produced. It's different today.

Goudy Oldstyle (Frederick W. Goudy, 1915) is complemented by the Rockwell Bold (Monotype Design Staff, 1934) headline. The slab serifs of the headline are in stark contrast to the tapering serifs of the body face.

Today, you, too, can look good in print

Not very long ago, preparing good-looking, high-quality documents was a costly and time-consuming process. And on top of all that, companies had minimal control over the documents they produced. It's different today.

ITC Clearface Regular (Victor Caruso, 1978, based on designs by Morris Fuller Benton, 1907) body text and Bodoni Poster Compressed (Morris Fuller Benton, 1910, based on designs by Giambattista Bodoni, 1798) headline work well together. Because of the narrow width of the headline, we were able to increase the point size substantially.

Today, you, too, can look good in print

Not very long ago, preparing good-looking, high-quality documents was a costly and time-consuming process. And on top of all that, companies had minimal control over the documents they produced. It's different today.

Clearface Gothic 65 Medium (Morris Fuller Benton, 1908) nicely complements the ITC Clearface Regular body text in this version.

As you have seen from the above examples, either serif or sans-serif headlines can be used with serif text, if discretion is used in selecting the headlines. Our body text was Oldstyle, Transitional or Modern. We were able to contrast with a sans serif that carried through with the feel of the body text or with a slab-serif headline, which offsets the bracketed serifs of the text.

When selecting headline type for a document, design a dummy that will give you all possible combinations of headline and text. Set up a style sheet and, basing one style upon another, change the base style. You will probably discover that the size of the headline type must change, depending upon the typefaces selected. Don't be afraid to experiment. Sometimes the best combinations of headline and text are those you are certain will not work.

Type in Boxes

When headline type or type for callouts is placed in boxes, whether deep boxes or bars, it must have enough space to breathe, but not so much that it looks lost. Of course, the amount of space around the type will depend upon the overall layout and upon the typeface itself.

This type is too crowded in the box.

Too little type for the box.

This type fits the box well.

Type placed inside boxes presents the challenge of properly sizing both the type and the box for the amount of copy that is there. It is particularly challenging when there is one line of type and a set layout to fill.

THIS TYPE
IS SET
TOO NARROW
TO HARMONIZE
WITH THE
BOX SHAPE

This type hugs the top of the box and fits uncomfortably

In both these cases, the type is too small for the box and doesn't take the box's constraints into consideration.

This type is sized properly for the box and fills the space appropriately without crowding

What is true of a filled box with reversed type is also true of an outlined box with positive type

Here we have filled the boxes with appropriately sized type. It appears comfortable inside its box.

As you see in these examples, when you place type in a box of any shape, you must allow for the shape and give the type enough room to breathe, although you don't want it to look like it has been abandoned in a vast empty area. Type should be centered in the box, visually, approximately equidistant from all sides.

Posters and Ads

Posters and ads are similar, inasmuch as the text, for the most part, takes up less space proportionately than in other documents. This is not to say that the text is unimportant. The text is often the meat of the poster or ad, and should be written powerfully, with added attention paid to the details of composition.

In the year that these posters were produced, Seacoast Repertory Theatre used type as the primary focus of the poster, with a single piece of art as accompanying imagery. The most important elements in the posters are the name of the play, the credits and the dates.

Often, because space is limited, we select type with a large number of characters per inch, such as Adobe Minion, for the body text in ads. Because we want the best possible appearance, it is a good idea to choose commercial fonts that have a sufficient number of built-in kerning pairs, in order to avoid having to do a lot of manual kerning.

The New England Center used a series of ads featuring lots of white space. This created the impression of a peaceful setting for meetings and conferences.

Drop Caps

Drop caps and *raised caps* — large capital letters used as the first character of an article — are a throwback to the illuminated letters that were once used in hand-lettered manuscripts. As is the case with other devices, the feature should be used with discretion. Overuse of drop caps and raised caps detracts from their value and makes them ordinary.

our score and seven years ago our fathers brought forth on this continent, a new nation, conceived in Liberty, and dedicated to the proposition that all men are created equal. Now we are engaged in a great civil war, testing whether that nation, or any nation so conceived and so dedicated, can long endure. We are met on a great battle-field of that war. We have come to dedicate a portion of that field, as a final resting place for those who here gave their lives that that nation might live.

This illuminated letter is representative of the drop-cap method used by scribes and others who tediously hand-lettered documents. Note how the illuminated letter sits, for the most part, in the left margin.

Four score and seven years ago our fathers brought forth on this continent, a new nation, conceived in Liberty, and dedicated to the proposition that all men are created equal. Now we are engaged in a great civil war, testing whether that nation, or any nation so conceived and so dedicated, can long endure. We are met on a great battle-field of that war. We have come to dedicate a portion of that field, as a final resting place for those who here gave their lives that that nation might live.

Drop caps are often used in documents. It is important to match the size and weight of the drop cap to the paragraph in which it resides, and to match the number of lines for the drop with the importance of the article. Note that the drop cap letter has been adjusted so its height is equal to the height of the ascenders on the line.

Four score and seven years ago our fathers brought forth on this continent, a new nation, conceived in Liberty, and dedicated to the proposition that all men are created equal. Now we are engaged in a great civil war, testing whether that nation, or any nation so conceived and so dedicated, can long endure. We are met on a great battle-field of that war. We have come to dedicate a portion of that field, as a final resting place for those who here gave their lives that that nation might live.

Raised caps are used more and more frequently — primarily because they are easier to make and can be set readily using any word processor, composition or illustration program. While they have their place, they lack the elegance of the drop cap.

Body Type

We have discussed the mechanics of body type at some length in previous chapters. When designing with type, particularly when designing documents using smaller amounts of body text, the text should be selected for its effectiveness in communicating the feel of the message to the audience. For example, you might use large type (16 or 18 pt.) with plenty of leading in a workbook for primary school children, and substantially smaller type (11 or 12 pt.) in workbooks for use with older children in elementary school. Other applications for larger type sizes might include cookbooks and publications designed to be read by older persons, whose sight may be failing.

Italic type is sometimes used to indicate longer passages of quoted material. Don't do it. Italic type is hard to read in large amounts. Consider, instead, indenting the quoted passage from both margins and setting it off with extra space above and below.

One device often employed is the use of "period" type. This use of type that reflects (or is supposed to reflect) a particular time can be effective, if an appropriate style is chosen. If an inappropriate style is selected — even though it may have been used in that time period — readability may suffer. Of course all considerations about the typeface's readability and legibility must be taken into consideration.

When writing about the "Roaring Twenties" one might be tempted to use an Art Deco style of type, such as ITC Avant Garde Gothic. Aside from the fact that it wasn't designed until 1970, this typeface is hard to read as body text.

Herb Lubalin and Tom Carnase designed Avant Garde Gothic in 1970. It's a wonderful typeface when used in larger sizes, but is difficult to read as body text because of the very wide round letters and even stoke weight.

When selecting a type style for books, magazines, newsletters and other longer documents, consider its overall readability and its character count. You can save hundreds or thousands of dollars simply by watching the character count (and hence the page count) for larger publications.

Character count was discussed in some detail in Chapter 4.

When choosing a text face for longer publications, be sure that the letterform is regular and without flourishes to ensure the greatest readability.

Compare the appearance and readability of these three typefaces. Similes are figures of speech explicitly comparing two apparently unlike things for the purpose of creating a heightened effect or emphasing a point.

Compare the appearance and readability of these three typefaces. Similes are figures of speech explicitly comparing two apparently unlike things for the purpose of creating a heightened effect or emphasing a point.

Compare the appearance and readability of these three typefaces. Similes are figures of speech explicitly comparing two apparently unlike things for the purpose of creating a heightened effect or emphasing a point.

Walbaum (top), adapted from Justus Erich Walbaum's 1803 work by Günter Gerhard Lange in 1985, exhibits strong thick and thin strokes that make reading long passages in this face tiring. Caxton (middle), designed by Leslie Usherwood in 1981, is very effective when used in small blocks of text or as display type; its unique letterform makes it less acceptable for long-running text. ITC New Baskerville (bottom), adapted from John Baskerville's 1757 design by the Linotype Design Staff in 1978, combines regular letterform with an easy-to-read x-height.

Type and Color

In Chapter 4, we briefly discussed the necessity of sufficient contrast between type and its background in order to ensure that the type is readable. Color issues go beyond contrast, however. While this is not a discussion of color per se, it is important to understand some color issues as they pertain to design.

Color has the power to elicit an emotional response from viewers. While some responses arise from personal or cultural experience, others are more nearly universal. Warm colors tend to stimulate, while cool colors relax most people. When designing for international distribution, it is important to recognize that certain colors (or shapes) can have negative connotations, while others are viewed positively.

When thinking of colors, you might want to group them. Use high-key color to grab attention. Earth tones will give a warm, comfortable feel to the piece. Soft pastels, such as lavender, light blue, green or yellow or peach, can be used to convey a pure feeling. Muted pastels, such as mauves and blue-grays, convey sophistication.

> *High-key colors include the additive and subtractive primaries and related colors, such as undiluted oranges and purples.*

Regardless of the color group in which you design a piece, it is important that your colors are harmonious. A high-key color in a piece with a muted-pastel color theme will look out of place and draw attention to itself. While this may sometimes be appropriate, you will want to experiment in order to produce exactly the effect you wish to achieve.

Be aware that using complementary colors — colors opposite one another on the color wheel — creates eyestrain. The colors clash with one another, sometimes even appearing to vibrate. So, placing magenta on green, blue on yellow, or red on cyan is not a good idea, unless you are trying to shock your audience.

When you select colors, remember that warm colors tend to reach out, while cool colors tend to recede. When working with type and colors, you may wish to emphasize or de-emphasize elements by selecting either warm or cool colors, and by placing them appropriately in the layout. Experiment with color, even with some effects that you are certain won't work. You may surprise yourself and produce a startling, but effective, combination.

Designing Logotypes

A logotype is, by definition, a logo made up entirely of type. The type may be given special treatment, or it may be combined with an image (or images) to enhance the impression it gives. Logotype design may range from a straightforward representation using a specific typeface or hand-drawn letterform to working with the type to achieve a specific effect.

Logotypes for the musical South Pacific (see earlier poster), Imaging and Design Center and Kid Ed. Note that while they all use logotypes, the graphic uses the type in different ways.

Interaction of Type and Graphics

When type and graphics appear together on a page, there is an automatic interaction. The interaction may be straightforward — some would say boring— or it may be inventive, perhaps even playful. In any case, the way type and graphics work together in a document sets the flavor for the document as a whole. Whatever treatment of type and graphics is chosen, the elements must work together as elements on the page. More important, they must work together within the limitations of the medium. These limitations are more readily apparent in printed documents than they are in documents for the Web.

Knocking Type Out of Photographs

Type is often knocked out or reversed out of photographs. When this process is used, the letters reveal the background beneath the photograph. If the photograph is process color and there is the slightest bit of misregistration, this will show up even in headlines. To avoid this, a trick that is often used is to print a narrow rule around each letter. This is most effectively done when the type has been converted to outlines, rather than working with live type.

A soft shadow was applied to the type here to allow it to be more visible against a similar-shade background.

Another trick to solve the problem of misregistration is to color the type with colors common to the background image. For example, if the type is reversed out of a blue, it could be tinted a lighter blue by using cyan and magenta. This would mask any effects of bad registration.

Nothing can compensate, however, for smaller text sizes that are reversed out of a photograph. When fonts with very thin strokes or hairlines are used, those areas will always fill in. Of course, text reversed out of a grayscale image will not have this problem, since it does not have to deal with more than one color of ink. The dot structure of the image, however, may make the type more difficult to read.

Overprinting type on a lighter background will avoid the problem of misregistration. If you do so, remember that overprinting colored type will alter the color. If type is to be overprinted on a photograph or colored background, the best solution is to use black type.

Unique Treatments of Display Type

Display type can be given a number of treatments that allow you to make a point not only with the words and style of type, but also with the manner in which you structure the headline.

A device frequently used for this purpose is placing type on a path. Paths can take on virtually any shape, from circles to freeform paths. Other treatments include using the mask or paste-inside feature to embed a picture in the headline, and to apply color and shading treatments.

ride the wave to success

ride the

WAVE

to success

Don't Let Your Benefits

FADE AWAY

These three display type treatments — type on a path, embedded images within the type and application of a graduated tint — are frequently used to add impact to headlines.

Working with Wraparounds

While type is often used above or below a photograph or another image, it may also wrap around the image. Most often, a wraparound is used on a squared-up photograph, where the photograph intersects a column of type. At other times type is wrapped around one or many sides of an image. Care must be taken to retain the readability of the type.

The three wraparounds below help us appreciate some pitfalls of this technique.

Whether we like it or not, one of the most important areas of nursing — regardless of areas of specialty — is keeping abreast of developments in the field. New drugs and new procedures are constantly brought out, and the nurse who is unaware of those changes is in a very precarious position. More and more frequently, as our professionalism is recognized by others in the medical community, our opinions are sought, and we are brought into the decision-making process. While this recognition that we are, indeed professionals is gratifying, it is not without risk. Reliance on yesterday's techniques and yesterday's products can as surely land a nursing professional in trouble as the same laxity can cause problems for physicians. In addition to the many seminars and conferences available to us, we can and should use the Internet to help us keep current on a regular basis.

A clipping path, applied in an image manipulation program such as Photoshop, allows certain areas of a photo to show. When type is set to run around a clipping path, it may flow into "holes" within the photo, as has happened here.

In this example, hyphenation was turned on and the clipping path, complete with the space between the report and the face, was left intact. This created a situation in which the type is very difficult to read.

Whether we like it or not, one of the most important areas of nursing — regardless of areas of specialty — is keeping abreast of developments in the field. New drugs and new procedures are constantly brought out, and the nurse who is unaware of those changes is in a very precarious position. More and more frequently, as our professionalism is recognized by others in the medical community, our opinions are sought, and we are brought into the decision-making process. While this recognition that we are, indeed professionals is gratifying, it is not without risk. Reliance on yesterday's techniques and yesterday's products can as surely land a nursing professional in trouble as the same laxity can cause problems for physicians. In addition to the many seminars and conferences available to us, the Internet to help us keep current on a regular basis.

Here the clipping path and hyphenation problems have been corrected, but because the type is treated as a single column, reading the information is choppy, at best.

Whether we like it or not, one of the most important areas of nursing — regardless of areas of specialty — is keeping abreast of developments in the field. New drugs and new procedures are constantly brought out, and the nurse who is unaware of those changes is in a very precarious position. More and more frequently, as our professionalism is recognized by others in the medical community, our opinions are sought, and we are brought into the decision-making process. While this recognition that we are, indeed professionals is gratifying, it is not without risk. Reliance on yesterday's techniques and yesterday's products can as surely land a nursing professional in trouble as the same laxity can cause problems for physicians. In addition to the many seminars and conferences available to us, we can and should use the Internet to help us keep current on a regular basis.

This is a much better solution. Type is broken into two columns, breaking around the nurse. The eye has a consistent starting point and does not need to jump over the graphic to continue the thought.

Another device, used less often but sometimes effective, is to reverse the wrap, so the type is inside the wrap area. This gives a shape to the type that, because of its lack of a consistent starting point, makes the type less easy to read. It is effective, though, as a means of presenting an argument graphically.

Watermelon... it makes you feel like a kid again, doesn't it? Just take that first bite, and think back to the good ol' days!

Type placed in the slice of watermelon follows the contour of the fruit.

Type and the Design Grid

The purpose of a design grid is to give a document structure. Essentially, it forces the reader's eye to follow the path of our choice. A grid, however, is not etched in stone. It may be broken by graphics or by the type itself.

> **The major force behind the design grid was the International Typographic Style or Swiss School of the 1950s. They were largely influenced by the Bauhaus.**

One example of breaking a grid with type occurs often in newsletters and magazines — the headline crossing a number of columns. The headline accomplishes several functions. First, it provides information about the following text. Second, it provides a structure for the following story. Third, and equally important from a design standpoint, it breaks up the page so there are no alleys from top to bottom.

Another way to add interest to a page by breaking the design grid is to use *callouts* — type taken from the text or introduced to make a point — that intersect more than one column.

When looking at the design of a publication, it is good to remember that most publications are viewed with facing pages visible. In most cases, the spread should present a cohesive whole. The spread should be balanced as to weight — without having one page very dark and the other very light. Of course, when the pages are unrelated, such as the opening page of an article in a magazine or a full-page ad, this is not an issue.

Often, when creating a spread, you will have headlines adjacent to one another. This should not present a problem if you have designed the pages with a wide enough inside margin. However, if the headlines compete, interfering with the understanding of the text, it may be necessary to change the typeface or type size of one of the headlines.

Your most important consideration, when using type and the design grid, is to ensure that the document is easy to read, and that your readers will be able to navigate easily. Whenever possible, you should avoid *jumps* — making your reader go to a nonsequential page to continue reading the article.

Summary

While there are, indeed, rules associated with the use of typography in a variety of documents, it is more important to use good sense. Remember the purpose of the headline, title or text, rather than slavishly following rules. Type can be used by itself in a number of interesting ways when creating headlines or logotypes, or it can be used in conjunction with graphics to create a more powerful effect. It should always be remembered, however, that most importantly: type is to read.

CHAPTER 7

Type and the Internet

As we have seen, the use of type in print gives us several options over which we have virtually limitless control. Today's communications, however, are not limited to pre-printed documents. Often readers seek information on the Internet, and then print it in their homes or offices, or they simply refer to an electronic document. We also create documents of a few or several hundred pages for download, or as electronic files that may accompany software as its manual.

In all these cases, we are presented with challenges and opportunities. While we are freed of many of the restraints of the printing press, such as concerns about registration and the cost of printing additional pages, we face the additional challenge of ensuring that our readers see the type, graphics and colors that we intend.

Displaying Type on Web Pages

The one certainty, when setting type for the Web, is that you face a high degree of variability. When you select fonts for a print project, as long as the output bureau uses the same fonts that you did when you created the document, you can rest assured that these fonts, in all their detail, will appear on the printed page.

At this stage in the evolution of the Internet, you can't make the same assumption when selecting typefaces for your Web pages. On the contrary, you can almost bet that what you're seeing on your monitor won't be the same as what users see when they view your site. At best, type selection and formatting on a Web page merely provides the viewer's browser with an idea of where the type should appear, at what point size, and in what typestyle.

Web pages are built with a markup language called "HTML" — an acronym for Hypertext Markup Language. From the standpoint of typography, HTML is primitive at best —the code presents many limitations. For example, you can surround a word with a tag telling the browser to display the enclosed text as italic, but you can't be sure what typeface or size the text will be.

The concept is straightforward. An *HTML tag* is code words (or letters) enclosed in brackets. Tags normally come in pairs. If you need to italicize a specific word, you just surround it with the appropriate tags (in this case <i> for italic and </i> to cancel the italic).

Golf is the most <i>difficult</i> game man has invented.

When the file is viewed in a browser, the HTML tag isn't displayed — it's interpreted. The word is italicized.

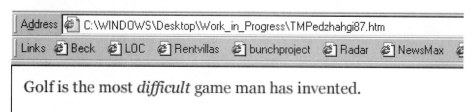

The browser dsplays the interpretation of the HTML code. In this instance, the word "difficult" was italicized.

There are two ways to display type on a Web page. The first way is as so-called "live" text. You can identify live text because you can select it by dragging the cursor over a word, phrase or story.

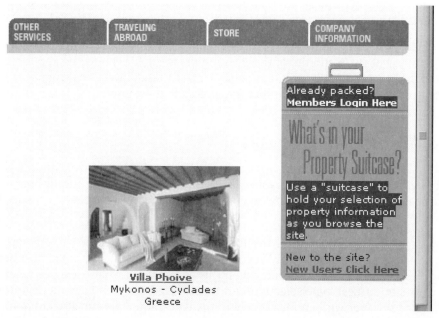

This text (from the Rentvillas.com site) has been selected. Notice that the phrase "What's in your Property Suitcase?" hasn't been selected — that's because it is a graphic, not live text.

The second way you can display words or phrases on your Web site is to create a graphic image that looks like type but is actually a picture. The advantage of displaying "type" in graphic form is that readers of the Web page don't need to have the font installed on their computers. The disadvantage is that it takes more time to load.

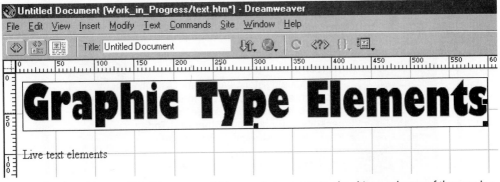

In this image from Macromedia's Dreamweaver Web-page design program, the object at the top of the page is a graphic object and the type at the bottom is live, regular text.

Type Elements You Can't Control

As mentioned, you must take into consideration a great deal of variability when you select type for the Web. Here are elements you can't control:

Default Font Size

The browser sets the default font size, so how large your live text elements appear is in the hands of the user. Let's reference a page from **http://www.ybor.org** — a well-designed Web site about Tampa's Ybor City (a historic Latin district in this central Florida city).

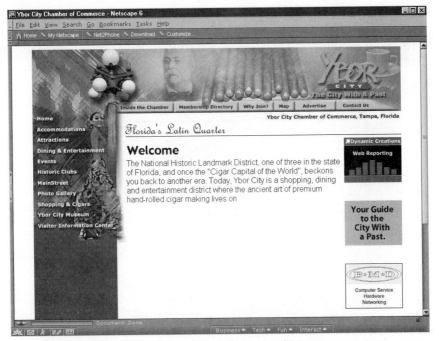

The default size of our browser font size was set to 12 pt. for viewing this image.

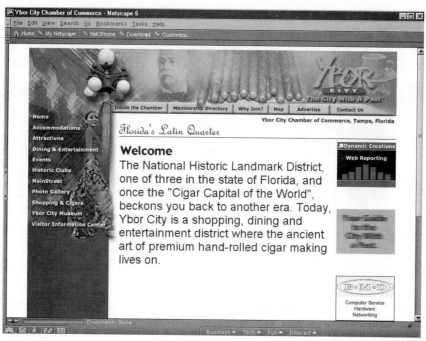

This is the same page with the default font size set to 150% of the default (also called the "basefont") browser size setting.

It is apparent that the designer had a smaller, more elegant look in mind. Unfortunately, if users set their default font size to something large (perhaps because their eyesight isn't what it was a few years ago), the feel of the page is completely changed.

Default Font Face

All major browsers provide a way for the user to select default fonts. You can spend all the time you want deciding which typeface best suits your design, but if the users don't have it installed on their computers, the font you chose won't display.

Most Web-design programs enable you to specify font and size attributes for text objects. In this example from Dreamweaver, we're selecting a sans-serif typeface for the top line of text.

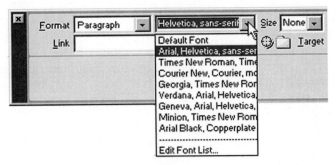

The selection — known as "alternative font sets" — displays not one, but a choice of three typefaces.

HTML supports what are known as "alternative font sets." If we want the bottom line to display in Georgia, and if the users have Georgia installed on their computers, everything will work as we wish. Failing that, however, the browser will use the next font in the font set — in this case, Times New Roman. If that font is not present on the user's computer, the default serif font as defined by the user's browser will be used.

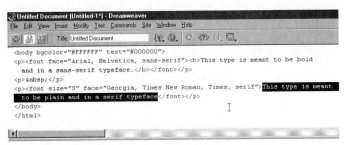

This screen capture shows the HTML code listing the alternative fonts. It is the result of the menu selection shown in the preceding image.

Screen Resolution

An additional complication arises because of the differences in resolution between Windows and Macintosh computers. The standard Windows resolution is 96 ppi (pixels per inch), while the Macintosh displays 72 ppi. The result of this difference is that the Macintosh displays type somewhat smaller than computers running Windows. Bear this difference in mind when you're designing your Web pages. Whichever platform you use to create your designs, remember to check your pages on the other(s) to ensure that the pages are equally readable and attractive at that resolution.

Comparing Web and Print Documents

If you have any experience designing and producing printed pages, particularly digital pages, then you've already had some experience with importing and positioning page elements. There are many parallels between putting objects onto printed pages and putting objects onto Web pages. There are also many differences between the two development environments.

The first, and arguably the most important, difference between designing for print and designing for the Web is the size of the page.

The Fold

A few short years ago, people were prophesying that few, if any, users would still be anchored to tiny 14-inch or 15-inch monitors. "Look at how prices are falling," they would say. "Why would anyone use a small monitor when you can buy a 17-inch or even a 21-inch display for a few hundred dollars?"

As is often the case with prophecies, the day foretold in the vision has come and gone. And, remarkably, many people are, in fact, still using 14-inch monitors. These monitors — and they're still by far the dominant display hardware — usually display an area that's 640 px. (pixels, or screen dots) × 480 px. To be safe, you might actually think in terms of 600 px. × 400 px., allowing yourself a bit of room just in case the viewer's monitor isn't perfectly adjusted, and to allow for the space that will be taken up by the browser's navigational tools.

600 pixels is wider than the printing area of a letter-size document. In order to allow the document to print (without cutting off words), we need to reduce the width to 535 pixels.

Take a moment to review the following image. Using a page from Against The Clock's *Macromedia Dreamweaver: Designing for the Web* book, we've superimposed a transparent frame that represents how much of a letter-sized page can be seen on a "standard" monitor at full magnification.

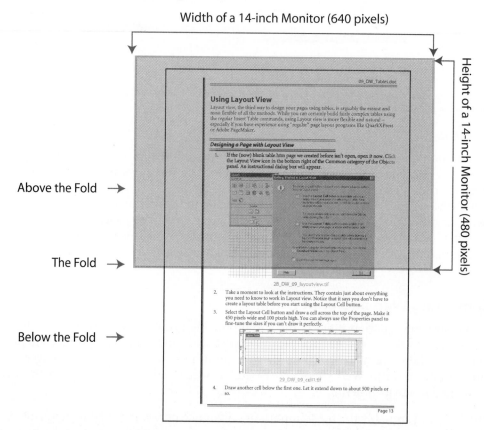

Width of a 14-inch Monitor (640 pixels)

Height of a 14-inch Monitor (480 pixels)

Above the Fold →

The Fold →

Below the Fold →

A page designed to be printed and read requires that you scroll vertically to see approximately half the page.

Notice the three labels on the left side of the illustration; they show what Web designers call the "fold" of a Web page (this is an allegory to the fold of a newspaper). The fold is the location at the bottom of a user's monitor below which additional content can't be seen without scrolling down. All users can see anything that is positioned above this fold — even on a 14-inch monitor. Anything below this region — unless a large monitor is used — cannot be seen without using the scroll bars on the right side of the browser window (or clicking a link to move down the page).

As an added twist, many Web pages will be downloaded and printed; 600 px. is wider than the print area of a letter-size document. In order to enable the document to print, we need to reduce the width to 535 px. As a rule, pages designed to be viewed online are likely to be home pages, menus, navigational pages and pages with large graphics.

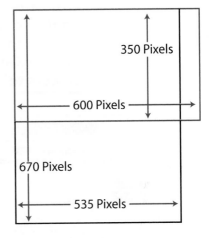

Pay attention to the width as well as the height of Web pages meant to be printed. The live area should not exceed the width the printer is capable of printing. The blue dimension here will fill the maximum safe area on most monitors. Use the black dimensions for pages that will print.

Contrast

As with pages designed for print, it is important to create visual contrast when designing pages for the Web. Not surprisingly, the trend of effective corporate sites — and even *Wired* magazine — is the use of black type on a white background. This sharply contrasts with the "artistic" approaches of electric type on black or patterned backgrounds. Color is effective, but only if there is adequate constrast and the result is not an assault on the eyes.

12-point Arial in black on a white background.
12-point Arial in red on a white background.
12-point Arial in green on a white background.
12-point Arial in blue on a white background.
12-point Arial in cyan on a white background.
12-point Arial in yellow on a white background.

12-point Arial in white on a blackbackground.
12-point Arial in red on a black background.
12-point Arial in green on a black background.
12-point Arial in blue on a black background.
12-point Arial in cyan on a black background.
12-point Arial in yellow on a black background

As you can see clearly in this example, some color combinations should not be used. Type that is hard to read will be ignored. Good contrast is essential.

Your Web page layout should exhibit a strong hierarchical approach, bearing in mind the way we read information — from the top down, and left to right. Consistency and predictability will keep users' interest and will encourage interaction with the message presented. Avoid a jumble of graphics and variable justification and provide strong direction as you establish a hierarchical approach.

Tables — a standard in HTML — enable you to exercise a considerable amount of control over page layout, including managing the width of a text region. Frames are another method used by designers to specify page designs.

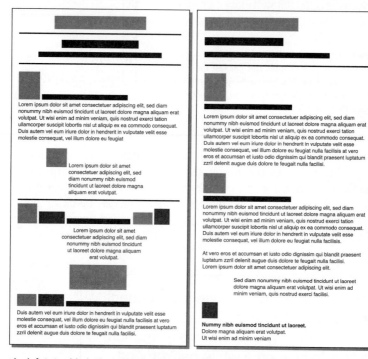

The design on the left is jumbled. The information is not easy to focus on, since there is no clearly defined hierarchical arrangement. The design on the right, however, promotes easy comprehension.

Underlining

It is also important to understand that, on the Web, underlined type is typically a hyperlink — clicking on the type takes you to another location. For this reason, you should never use underlined text for emphasis; you will confuse your readers. When the text is a hyperlink, however, it is best to create a meaningful link:

Use: Register for the <u>Home Design Show</u>.

Instead of: To register for the Home Design Show, <u>click here</u>.

As is the case when producing type for print, type in ALL CAPITALS is more difficult to read than type in lowercase letters. As we read pages, our eye is trained to recognize shapes — such as those formed by the use of upper- and lowercase letters. Copy set entirely in uppercase results in a rectangular shape, which is much harder for the eye to distinguish. Note the following examples.

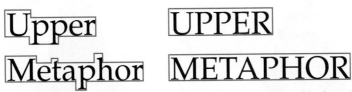

Here, the ascenders and descenders give words containing lowercase letters discernible shape. They are easier to read than the blocks of uppercase letters.

For our purposes, there are four types of letters: vertical, curved, a combination of vertical and curved, and oblique. The upper halves of letters are easier to read than the lower halves. To maintain a flow of reading use *sentence case* (only the first word and proper nouns are capitalized) instead of initial caps.

Readability and character flow

As you see from this example, characters are more easily recognized from the top half of the letters than from the bottom half.

Anti-aliasing

When you're creating type for the Web — particularly graphic type objects created in an imaging application like Adobe Photoshop or Macromedia Fireworks — you can take advantage of a technique called "anti-aliasing." Anti-aliasing is used to smooth the appearance of type on the screen. Without this technique, certain fonts may look jagged.

Anti-aliasing softens the edge of graphic type characters by mixing colors at the edge of each letterform. Here are four different anti-alias settings from an Adobe Photoshop type object. The one on the left is the original letterform — without the technique applied. As you move from left to right, the degree of the effect applied increases.

The letter on the left has no anti-aliasing applied. As you move from left to right, the degree of anti-aliasing applied increases.

Look more closely, and you'll really see the effect. The more anti-aliasing you apply, the fuzzier the edge appears when magnified; the theory is that at regular size the type appears much smoother. It works — to a point.

This enlargement of oblique type that is not anti-aliased (left) and type that is anti-aliased (right) shows that although the letter appears smoother, the effect is created by adding zones of gray, softening the image.

When type is anti-aliased, it retains more of its character than does type where anti-aliasing is not applied. But it can result in overly soft type. At smaller sizes, it's probably a good idea not to apply anti-aliasing. The general rule you should follow is that if it looks hard to read, it is hard to read. Use common sense and a critical eye when analyzing the readability of your Web pages.

Serif type loses its character and distinction. (antialiased)

Serif type loses its character and distinction. (not antialiased)

Sans-serif type is easier to read. (antialiased)

Sans-serif type is easier to read. (not antialiased)

Italic type is difficult to read because of jaggies. (antialiased)

Italic type is difficult to read because of jaggies. (not antialiased)

From these examples, you can see which type best retains its character and is easiest to read. For this reason, you will often alter the specifications of print documents when translating them for the Web.

Fonts and Font Specification

As we have pointed out, specifying type for print is straightforward. Once the document is printed, everyone is able to view the font. On the Web, however, readers must have the font active on their computer if they are to experience what the designer intended.

Microsoft Core Fonts for the Web

One way to ensure that a reasonable variety of fonts is available is to use Microsoft's free Core Fonts for the Web, which are available at http://www.microsoft.com/typography/fontpack/default.htm. These fonts are included with all Microsoft products for Windows and are available for download for both Windows and Macintosh systems.

Andale Mono
Arial Regular, *Italic*, **Bold**, ***Bold Italic***, **Black**
Comic Sans, **Sans Bold**
Courier New, *Italic*, **Bold**, ***Bold Italic***
Georgia Regular, *Italic*, **Bold**, ***Bold Italic***
Impact
Times New Roman, *Italic*, **Bold**, ***Bold Italic***
Trebuchet MS, *Italic*, **Bold**, ***Bold Italic***
Verdana Regular, *Italic*, **Bold**, ***Bold Italic***
Webdings

The Microsoft Core Fonts for the Web are a free download for both Windows and Macintosh and ship with the current version of Microsoft Explorer.

- **Andale Mono** (formerly named Monotype.com, 1997), 1999, Monotype Typography.

- **Arial**, 1990, Monotype Design Staff.

- **Comic Sans**, 1995, Vincent Connare. This face is based on lettering from comic magazines.

- **Courier New**, 1990, originally designed as a typewriter face for IBM and redrawn by Adrian Frutiger for the IBM Selectric series.

- **Georgia**, 1996, Matthew Carter.

- **Impact**, 1965, Geoffrey Lee. Impact is a trademark of Stephenson Blake (Holdings) Ltd.

- **Times New Roman**, 1932, Monotype Design Department. Designed for *The Times of London* newspaper.

- **Trebuchet MS**, 1996, Vincent Connare. Trebuchet uses design features of the sans serifs of the 1930s, with a large x-height and round features intended to promote readability on signs.

- **Verdana**, 1996, Matthew Carter.

- **Webdings**, 1997, Microsoft's Vincent Connare and Monotype designers Sue Lightfoot, Ian Patterson and Geraldine Wade.

While having 10 font families fairly universally available and free is a start, it does not satisfy the desires of most designers to provide unique typographic solutions for their clients. This is of particular concern to many Macintosh users (for years the primary designers of Web sites), who routinely use PostScript fonts for print production. Now Macintosh users find that they must also provide Windows users (who typically use TrueType) the ability to access the typeface. It is still important, therefore, to take into consideration the fonts common to each platform

Windows 98, 12 pt. type	Macintosh, 12 pt. type
Arial	**Chicago**
Arial Black	Courier
Arial Narrow	Geneva
Arial Rounded MT Bold	Helvetica
Book Antiqua	Monaco
Bookman Old Style	New York
Century Gothic	Palatino
Century Schoolbook	Times
Courier New	
Garamond	For those who have laser printers:
MSLineDraw	Avant Garde Gothic
Tahoma	Bookman
Times New Roman	New Century Schoolbook
Verdana	

Standard typefaces on the Windows and Macintosh platforms are different. Care must be taken in typeface specification. Note that type on the Macintosh appears smaller.

Specifying Type in HTML

As already mentioned, HTML specifications provide alternative font lists in order to accommodate the availability of different fonts on a variety of computers. Type from both Windows and Macintosh platforms should be included in the specification to ensure consistency of design.

This raises some problems, if the designer intends to cause lines to break in a specific way, because each font has its own metrics, which causes variable line breaks. For the most part, though, variable line breaks are acceptable.

As is the case with desktop publishing and word processing, using today's relatively sophisticated Web-page-creation programs makes selecting the font for Web pages virtually transparent. Simply select an appropriate typeface, and then select a style and size from the menu. The code is written automatically, with a minimum of errors.

Specifying Face

As we have discussed, if the type specified is to be displayed, it must be resident on the user's computer. For that reason, a font set is usually generated. A font set should include fonts common to both Windows and Macintosh platforms.

<arial, helvetica, sans-serif>

This specification calls for Arial (common to Windows), Helvetica (common to the Macintosh) and the user's default sans-serif font if neither of the preceding are available.

If core fonts, such as Arial, Helvetica, Times New Roman and Times are called, of if other fonts from the Core Fonts for the Web collection are requested, there is a probability that at least one of the fonts will be resident on most computers.

Specifying Size

While we are used to specifying type in point sizes when preparing print documents, specifying type for the Web is much different. Specifying type in print, we might indicate Helvetica 12/15.

In Web typesetting, the *basefont size* is the browser default. Body text is set in sizes of 1-7, which are defined in relation to this basefont size. One method used to alter the size of the type relative to the basefont size is to specify it using relative values, such as the tag <font size=+2> or <font size=–2>.

Headings are specified as sizes H1 through H6, with H1 being the largest. It is a good idea to avoid very large headline sizes, since they can look clunky.

The values 1–7, for both the body font and for headings, correspond to printed type point sizes. Most browsers have adopted the original Mosaic/Netscape sizes, although the precise specification is left to the developers of browsers, and to the user, who defines the physical size of the basefont; the size is further affected by platform. Based on a default size of 12, the type sizes are as follows:

Font Size	Point Size	Heading #
1	8	H6
2	10	H5
3	12	H4
4	14	H3
5	18	H2
6	24	H1
7	36	

Using this chart gives you a reasonable hint as to what sizes you are dealing with, when using the default of Font Size 3 = Point Size 12.

While leading (line spacing) is specified when preparing type for print, it is unspecified and relative to the point size on the Web. This is similar to allowing type specified for print to default to the "automatic" leading of 120% of point size.

Specifying Color

Color is specified by using the HTML specifications #RRGGBB with 00 equaling no part of the color and FF equaling 255 parts of the color. Green type, for example, could be specified using the tags:

```
<font color="#00FF00">
Green type here
</font>
```

Because Windows computers and Macintoshes have different color palettes, there are 216 colors that appear consistently on both platforms; these are called "Web-safe colors." To ensure Web-safe colors, only use 00, 33, 66, 99, CC, FF in the R, G or B specifications, if you type them instead of selecting a color from a palette. Each increment is equal to 51 units (20%) of the color scale. Since the designation is applied to each color (red, green and blue), there are a total of 216 colors (6^3). Most major graphics applications, such as Macromedia Dreamweaver, Microsoft FrontPage, Adobe Photoshop and Macromedia Flash, offer Web-safe palettes to ensure that your designs will encompass only these colors.

Websafe Colors						
Designation	00	33	66	99	CC	FF
RGB Amount	0	51	102	153	204	255
Percentage	0	20	40	60	80	100

The Web-safe colors represent only a very small range of colors available in the full RGB spectrum.

Using Special Characters

One other consideration in Web-page type is the use of special characters like single (') and double ("") quotation marks, known as "typographers quotes," apostrophes, copyright symbols, em dashes (—) and others.

Let's look at quotes. We've discussed the proper use of typographer's quotes in printed materials. It's a bit trickier to achieve the proper characters on your Web pages, but well worth the effort.

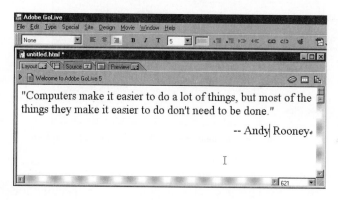

Here's a quote from famous humorist Andy Rooney. You can see two typographic errors. The quote is enclosed by inch marks, and the author's name is preceded by two regular dashes (-) instead of the proper em dash (—).

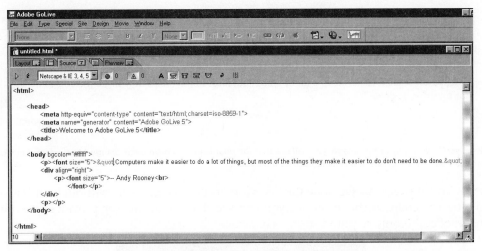

If you look at the HTML code, you'll see that the standard tag for inch marks is confused with what we know to be proper quote marks.

To display true typographer's quotes or other special characters, you have to change the code. Professional designers pay a great deal of attention to such details — it shows in their work. Since you're already fighting an uphill battle in controlling type display on your Web sites, at the minimum you need to gain control over anything that you can. Special characters are a sign of high-quality detailing on the part of the design and development team.

Since you cannot type the characters directly from the keyboard, as you're used to doing with print type, it's best to be aware of the code. If the text editor you are using doesn't provide you with the selection of special characters (often in a menu or palette) that you need, you can insert these yourself. Here's the code for opening and closing double and single quotes:

Opening Double Quote	"	&#147
Closing Double Quote	"	&#148
Opening Single Quote	'	&#145
Opening Quote	'	&#146

```
<body bgcolor="#ffffff">
   <p><font size="5">&#147;Computers make it easier to do a lot of things, but most of the things they make it easier to do don't need to be done.&#148;</fc
<div align="right">
   <p><font size="5">-- Andy Rooney<br>
```

To fix the code in this example, we simply replace the &quot with the code for the correct characters.

When you display the page in a browser window, the difference is immediately apparent. This is the way the page should look — inch marks are a glaring error to anyone who understands type, whether it's on the Web or on the side of a milk carton.

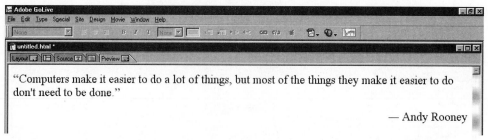

"Computers make it easier to do a lot of things, but most of the things they make it easier to do don't need to be done."

— Andy Rooney

When you look closely at this image, you will see that the double primes have been changed to quotation marks and the double hyphen has been changed to an em dash.

Many layout programs facilitate the insertion of special characters without your having to alter the code. In this example, you can see that Dreamweaver provides an entire menu of commonly required special characters.

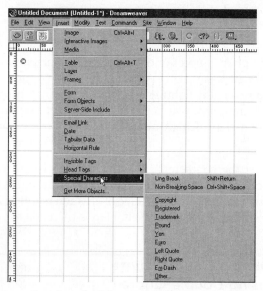

The copyright character, among others, is available from Dreamweaver's Insert menu.

If the special character you need isn't available from a menu, most applications also provide a way to pick the character from a grid. When you do, the programs will generate the proper HTML code tag automatically to ensure that the character will display on your visitors' browsers. Fortunately these special characters are part of the standard ASCII character set — the standard definition of fonts like Times, Helvetica, Geneva and other standard Web fonts.

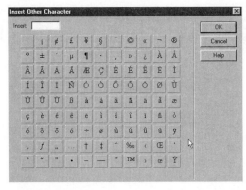

Additional characters that are part of the standard ASCII character set can be accessed from a grid in most Web creation programs.

Here are a few more of the most common special characters you might need when developing your sites:

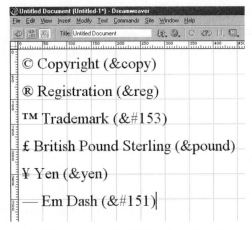

Often it's easier to simply insert special characters in the HTML string rather than peruse a list or grid. Knowing the common (and often understandable) hardcode makes tweaking a page easier and faster.

Headings

Because headings are important, we often want them to appear in a unique font. Since readers must have the font on their computer, this creates some complications. We may want to set a heading in a unique type style, only to be foiled by the default fonts of the person viewing the page.

DELPHIAN Bodoni

Swing Bold

Since we have these TrueType fonts on our system, we can specify them.

Delphian **Bodoni**
Swing Bold

This substitution identifies the intent of the designer, but it certainly doesn't display the nuance of expression that was intended. As a result of this limitation, headings are often prepared as GIF files. While this allows the designer to control the appearance of the heading, it presents some additional challenges.

GIF files (Graphics Interchange Format) are graphics saved as indexed color or grayscale images; they have a maximum of 256 colors or shades of gray.

Although a GIF can be saved with transparency, which is desirable when it is displayed against a background of variable color, transparent GIFs sometimes have undesirable artifacts. A GIF file, since it is artwork instead of a font, can also take an unreasonably long time to load. Several headings (graphics) on a page can make the page load so slowly that the reader will click away to another source of information or product.

Styles

Thus far, we've been using the term "style" to refer to attributes applied to individual characters, words, phrases or paragraphs. Unfortunately, the use of the term style can lead to confusion — especially when you're new to setting type on Web pages or HTML in general.

The term "styles" as it relates to formatting, such as bold or italic, predates Web development, and originated in the early days of typesetting. As word-processing and page-layout programs appeared, the term "style" began to take on the new meaning of "style sheets." *Style sheets* are formatting instructions that control character formatting, paragraph formatting, positioning, page-break information and more.

Think about how documents are structured, particularly lengthy documents. Longer documents — and Web pages certainly fall into this category — are organized into editorial priority with headings and subordinate headings. You can see such editorial priority in action with style sheets, for example, in this course. There's a primary heading, which is the name of the chapter. Underneath that main heading, there are secondary headings, which break the chapter into logical sections.

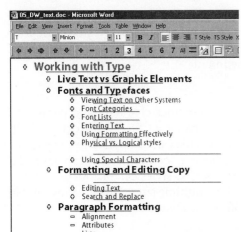

As in this example from another Against The Clock (ATC) book, each paragraph and copy element in ATC courses is assigned a style sheet. This ensures consistency and enables us to make global changes to any style in the document. The outline, showing levels of headlines, is on the left; the resulting text is on the right.

Many of the secondary headings have headings underneath them, and in some cases, there's actually a fourth heading. Each heading has a specific format applied — font, size, color, space before and after, and page-break information — contained in its own style sheet. These style sheets contain all the formatting attributes we defined before we started writing this book. HTML treats headings in the same way in which we treated them in this outline, by defining and structuring the content.

Headings aren't the only elements in the ATC course or on a Web page that are assigned a style sheet. Each element — body text, bulleted lists, unnumbered lists, captions and sidebar text, for example — is assigned a style sheet.

Types of Styles

There are two types of style sheets in use today. The first is known as "HTML styles" and the second as "Cascading Style Sheets," or "CSS." Both enable you to combine formatting attributes to create and identify a style. Once this style has been defined, it can be applied to any text object with a single click.

> **HTML 4.0 specifications state that you shouldn't use HTML styles; instead, use Cascading Style Sheets. While more powerful, CSS isn't supported by earlier browsers. HTML styles are more limited than Cascading Style Sheets, but are supported by all browsers.**

HTML Styles

HTML styles are older, and they're not as robust as CSS style sheets. You can use character and paragraph attributes to build an HTML style and apply it manually to any text, but changing the style doesn't change every item to which it was already attached. Nor does modifying an existing HTML style change incidences of that style throughout your site. When you save a style sheet, HTML styles are stored in your root folder under the name Styles.xml. You can load this file into another document if you want to use the same styles in another document.

Cascading Style Sheets, or CSS

A newer form of style sheets, CSS also contains and defines character and paragraph attributes, but offers a marked difference; when you change a CSS — any text to which it was assigned changes to reflect the new attributes. This can be applied to the page or throughout an entire site. Using CSS is a more flexible technique and can save you considerable time by comparison with HTML styles. CSS styles can be independent of a single site — the same set of styles can be used by multiple sites and can allow global changes to those sites through the modification of the shared styles.

Not all browsers support CSS, and those that do don't necessarily handle them correctly. For the most part, Web designers largely agree that the oldest browsers they're willing to address are Internet Explorer 4.x and Netscape Navigator 4.x.

Fonts Embedded in Documents

A solution to the challenge we face with font availability is to embed fonts in the document. While this is easily accomplished in print documents, and particularly with PDF, it's a little trickier to embed fonts in Web pages.

As of September 2001, current-level browsers do not support TrueDoc, although some older browsers do.

Macintosh Internet Explorer users can use embedded fonts only if they have been created using CSS, not using the font face HTML command.

First, fonts need to be converted from their native Type 1 (PostScript), TrueType or OpenType formats into an embeddable format. As you might suspect, there are two competing formats for embeddable type:

- **Embedded Open Type** (.eot), developed by Microsoft and Adobe

- **TrueDoc** (.pfr), developed by Netscape and Bitstream

Of course, not just any font can be embedded. Some fonts have their permissions set to "no embedding." Others are noted as previewable — they can be used on static Web pages, but should not be used on interactive pages. The embedding levels of fonts can be checked on Windows computers by using Microsoft's free font properties extension. As of this writing, the Macintosh does not have an equivalent tool for determining whether or not a font can be embedded into a page.

This font can be legally embedded.

 This is a Windows core font and doesn't need to be embedded.

 This font cannot be embedded either for legal reasons or because the font is broken.

The icons indicating ability to be embedded are traffic light green, yellow and red. If a font carries the "no embedding" icon, an embeddable version may be available from the font's vendor.

If you choose to create Embedded Open Type, you begin by downloading and installing Microsoft's free Web Embedding Fonts Tool (WEFT) for Windows. If you plan to produce TrueDoc fonts, you must purchase Bitstream's WebFont Wizard or WebFont Maker for Windows or Macintosh.

Embedded fonts are not actually installed on the user's system so users are unable to utilize them for purposes other than those you have intended. The embedded fonts are used by the browser and are functional only for viewing specific Web pages. In fact, you can choose to subset or embed only the characters you have used, resulting in a smaller file size. (This is particularly useful if you use a font only for main headings.)

You can subset your fonts on a per-page basis, so that each font object uses only the characters utilized for a particular page and is linked only to that page. You can opt to subset your font across all pages of your site, with the font object linked to all pages on the site that use it. You can choose to subset on the basis of an entire type family, which is beneficial when there is dynamic HTML on pages. There are other forms of subsetting that are also available, depending upon the program you use.

Summary

Although there are a number of challenges involved with typography on the Web, we have available to us the tools to provide a high level of typography that users with up-to-date browsers can appreciate. Tools such as Cascading Style Sheets and the ability to embed fonts are allowing the Web to be the publishing medium — or information highway — that has been envisioned for some years.

CHAPTER 8

The Mechanics of Type

We have already discussed a number of mechanical aspects of type. In Chapter 2, *Type Basics*, we explored type anatomy, learned how to copy fit and noted some differences in the basic character sets on Windows and Macintosh systems. In Chapter 3, *Exploring Categories of Type*, we analyzed letterforms, discussed the measuring systems for type and reviewed how to measure type vertically. In Chapter 4, Understanding the *Elements of Type*, we explored horizontal measurement and fit.

When we hit the print button, we expect that what we see on the monitor will closely resemble what is printed. Sometimes, however, we are rudely awakened by a font appearing in Courier, in a bitmapped rendition or with some other nuance that we know that we would never have intentionally created. In this chapter, we'll examine font technology, the components of fonts, how they are named and how we can manage them effectively both on our computers and in the printing process.

Fonts in Common Use

Type used today is generally either PostScript (Type 1) or TrueType. As more fonts are designed using the Open Type format, it will become dominant in the industry. Given the range of type available, it is useful to understand fonts' construction, technology, strengths and weaknesses.

In addition to their accustomed use, fonts can be embedded in documents. There are four possible embedding settings:

- **Installable embedding**. Fonts may be embedded in documents and permanently installed on the computer receiving the document.

- **Editable embedding**. Fonts may be embedded in documents, but must be installed only temporarily on the computer receiving the document.

- **Print and Preview embedding**. Fonts may be embedded in documents, but must be installed only temporarily on the computer receiving the document. Documents can only be opened as "read only."

- **Restricted License embedding**. Fonts may not be embedded in documents.

PostScript Fonts

PostScript fonts have two distinct parts: the *printer font*, which is an outline and is ultimately stored in the output device, and the *screen font*, which is a bitmap and is stored in the workstation. Both parts of the font must be resident on the system to print a document containing a PostScript font.

Both screen and printer fonts must be present if the PostScript font is to print correctly.

Most PostScript fonts ship with a few sizes of screen fonts and the one printer font. In the years before Adobe Type Manager, type displayed on the monitor would look terrible unless it was the exact size of one of the screen fonts. "Jaggies" were obvious and got in the way of good typography.

> **In the days before ATM, type would look bad on screen and visual kerning was almost an impossibility. However, the type printed.**

Adobe created a utility program, Adobe Type Manager (ATM), to link the bitmapped screen font to the outline printer font. The result is that PostScript fonts display correctly at any size.

ATM Deluxe, an enhancement of ATM, allows the operator to group fonts into sets. The sets may be turned on or off, resulting in a shorter font list. In addition, it will accurately render the *font metrics* (font height and width) of typefaces not available to the system, provided they are in ATM's database. ATM references its database, then applies the data to two Multiple Master fonts, serif and sans serif. The two master fonts are then sized to approximate the horizontal and vertical space as well as the weight of the font referenced.

When a part of a PostScript font is missing, the font prints or displays incorrectly. When the printer font is missing, the printer prints the document using the bitmap font. When the screen font is also missing, the printer uses the system's default font, usually the dreaded Courier.

As a font is expanded or condensed, it loses some of its character. The relationship between thick and thin strokes is distorted, and the font loses the distinguishing characteristics, which were designed into it. Multiple Masters are a superset of Post-Script fonts.

Type i   Type i
Type i   Type i

Notice how the normal font (above) distorts when it is condensed, as opposed to the manner in which the Multiple Master keeps the look and feel of the original design. The font used is ITC Avant Garde Gothic, a font with a single-weight stroke. See how the crossbar of the T looks thicker than the balance of the letter in the artificially condensed version. Note the effect on the p and e. The multiple master keeps a single stroke weight.

Multiple Master fonts can be expanded and condensed without distorting the relationships between the strokes. Fonts can also be made bolder or thinner in very precise increments. Some fonts can have other effects applied, such as skewing, without detracting from the overall design of the font. The varieties achievable are called "instances."

TrueType

Apple developed this font technology, in conjunction with Microsoft. Instead of relying on separate screen and printer fonts, TrueType generates its screen image from the printer font. The font's image is stored as a mathematical description of the character, constructed from a series of points. Because the screen image is generated from the printer font, and two parts of a font don't have to be linked, it isn't necessary to use a utility program to render the font properly on the monitor.

Some service providers will not accept jobs using TrueType fonts. If this is true in your case, find another service provider.

The screen and printer font information is contained in one element when using TrueType technology.

Open Type

Developed jointly by Microsoft and Adobe, the Open Type font format is a superset of TrueType and Type 1 fonts. It is designed to provide users with a simple way to install and use fonts, whether the fonts contain TrueType or PostScript outlines. Open Type fonts may be rasterized using Adobe Type Manager or a TrueType rasterizer. The user is unaware of what goes on behind the scenes, or of which outline format was used to design the font.

Rasterization is the process of converting outlines (vector images, such as type) into bitmaps so they can be printed. Printers, no matter what their resolution, ultimately print only bitmapped (raster) images.

Open Type, utilizing Unicode, handles large character sets.

Open Type provides the following:

- Broader multiplatform support

- Better support for international character sets

- Better protection for font data

- Smaller file sizes to make font distribution more efficient

- Broader support for advanced typographic control

These fonts facilitate the handling of large character sets using Unicode encoding. This allows for better international support and support for more typographic glyphs, such as ligatures and oldstyle characters. In addition, the digital signatures carried by Open Type fonts allow operating systems and browsers to identify the source and integrity of the font file. This includes fonts embedded in Web documents. Font designers can encode embedding restrictions into Open Type fonts that cannot be altered.

Font embedding restrictions for TrueType and PostScript fonts can be altered using programs such as Macromedia Fontographer.

Naming Fonts

Knowing how to name fonts is important only if you are going to create a font using a program such as Fontographer or IKARUS. The internal workings of fonts happen behind the scenes. Information about the internal workings of a font is contained in the font dictionary. Information that appears in the font dictionary is used by the PostScript interpreter to render the font correctly, or it may be used for informational purposes only, as you see in the list below. Some font dictionary entries include:

> **The *font dictionary* is code contained "inside" the font. Some of the information is accessible using Adobe Type Manager or Microsoft's TTF Properties tool. Some of the information is available only when using advanced developer's tools. To use fonts properly you don't need to know any of this internal information.**

- **FontType.** This required entry tells where the information for character descriptions is found and how it is represented.

- **FontMatrix.** This required entry transforms the character coordinate system into the user coordinate system.

- **FontName.** This optional entry is for information only, and may contain no spaces.

- **FontInfo.** This is an optional subdictionary.

- **Encoding.** This required entry gives the array of names necessary for character encoding.

- **FontBBox.** This required entry defines each character's bounding box.

- **UniqueID.** This optional entry is the number that uniquely identifies the font.

- **CharStrings.** This required entry associates keys with shape descriptions.

The FontInfo dictionary contains useful information about the font, the primary components of which are the FamilyName and the FullName.

- **FamilyName.** All fonts that make up a group of type based on the same design; for example Novarese, Helvetica, Clearface.

- **FullName.** The full name of an individual font. It usually begins with the FamilyName and then includes descriptive information, such as Novarese Book Italic.

- **Weight.** The parameter of the FullName that describes the heaviness of the font. In the case of Bookman Medium Italic this parameter would be "Medium."

- **ItalicAngle.** The angle in degree counterclockwise from the vertical.

- **UnderlinePosition.** Recommended position from the baseline for rendering an underline.

- **UnderlineThickness.** Recommended stroke weight for rendering an underline.

- **IsFixedPitch**. When this Boolean operative is true, the font is monospaced, like Courier. A *Boolean operative* is a mathematical expression in which each of the operands and the result take one of two values.

- **Version**. Version number of the font program.

- **Notice**. Trademark or copyright notice.

As you see, the FontInfo dictionary contains a lot of information that is valuable in identifying the font. Every font must have a unique FullName. If the FullName were not unique, the wrong font could be sent to the printer. If the metrics (the width of letters) were not identical, the document would print improperly. Often font vendors will build their distinctive identification into the FontName, such as Baskerville BE (Berthold), to ensure that the FullName is not duplicated by another font on the system.

The FontName is a condensed version of the FullName. The FontName must use a maximum of 64 ASCII characters and can include no spaces. Menu names can be different from the actual FontName. For example, the FontName can contain no spaces, while the Menu name may contain spaces.

Font Matching

If a font is missing, page-layout programs usually give you the option of selecting a font to replace it. Your replacement font can be permanent or temporary. This process is called "font mapping."

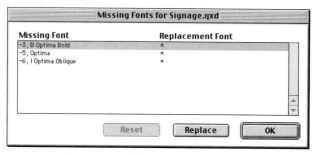

Font mapping dialog box for QuarkXPress.

The font mapping mechanism under Windows looks for installed fonts. If the font called isn't installed, Windows uses a font it thinks is similar — which is often in the same galaxy, but not close to what is requested. As an example, Wingdings is substituted if Symbol isn't present. This is understandable at one level, since they're both symbol fonts, but doesn't convey the designer's intent at all since the symbols are completely dissimilar.

Alternating lines of Symbol and Wingdings show the 96 keyboard characters in uppercase and lowercase.

The font metrics file built into the Windows Printer Description (.WPS) varies on a printer-by-printer basis, and may change if the target printer changes. This is an annoying problem since the files are supposed to be device-independent. Device-independent files should be able to be used on any printer and produce the same result. Because the font metrics of a Windows file change on a printer-by-printer basis, the layout of a document may change arbitrarily.

Software applications use either the font menu name or the PostScript FontName reference for matching. Printing options allow the substitution of PostScript for TrueType.

The Macintosh uses font ID numbers to match fonts, which are supposed to be unique. If Apple's guidelines for assigning IDs were followed, there would rarely be a problem. This, however, is not the case. For example, all roman fonts should have ID numbers lower than 16384. Font IDs range from 0 to 1677215 ($2^{24}-1$). UniqueID numbers for Type 1 fonts are controlled — Adobe maintains a registry of them. Additionally, the numbers between 4000000 and 4999999 are reserved for use in closed environments, such as fonts designed for use only within a corporation. These fonts cannot be registered. As an example, ABC company designs ABC Serif, a font for internal corporate use only.

As is true of Windows, the font menu name and the PostScript FontName are assumed to be identical.

The PANOSE Typeface Matching System allows font vendors to assign PANOSE numbers to their fonts. The application then embeds that number The PANOSE number is based on values describing visual characteristics of the fonts, such as x-height, midline, letterform, stroke variation and other features. The system substitutes an available font with the closest PANOSE number.

Font Matching Preferences

◇ ATM™ font matching
◆ PANOSE™ font substitution

Substitution tolerance: 50

Exact   Normal   Loose

Default font: Courier

☑ Show matching results

┌ Information ─────────────────────┐
│ Missing fonts will be substituted using PANOSE™. │
│ If there is no match within the specified tolerance, the Default │
│ font will be used. │
└──────────────────────────────────┘

OK
Cancel
Spellings...
Exceptions...
Help...

Alternate Spellings

Macintosh name:	Windows name:
American Typewriter	AmericanTypewriter
Brush Script	BrushScript
Century Old Style	CenturyOldStyle
Cooper Black	CooperBlack
Freestyle Script	FreestyleScript
Friz Quadrata	FrizQuadrata
H Franklin Gothic	Heavy FrGothHeavy
Letter Gothic	LetterGothic
Lubalin Graph	LubalinGraph
New Century Schlbk	NewCenturySchlbk

OK
Cancel
Add...
Edit...
Remove

The PANOSE font substitution window from PageMaker 6.5 allows the user to define a substitution tolerance and default font. Specific substitutions can be entered in the Exceptions menu. The alternate spellings are standard cross-platform Macintosh to Windows spellings.

Adobe Type Manager (ATM) can be used for on-screen substitution. ATM substitutes the Adobe Sans multiple master or the Adobe Serif multiple master for the missing font. This conveys the general look, but is certainly not a substitute for the real font.

Managing Fonts on the Computer

If you have just a few fonts, managing them is no problem. Just install them in the Fonts folder within the System folder (Macintosh) or in the Fonts folder (Windows), and use them. When you have hundreds or even thousands of fonts, however, you spend most of your time scrolling through menus if you use this method. On top of that, the Macintosh limits the number of fonts you can place in the Fonts folder, so you can't torture yourself in this fashion.

When working with a large number of fonts, we recommend using Adobe Type Manager Deluxe (Windows or Macintosh), Font Reserve or Suitcase (Macintosh) to turn your fonts on and off as necessary. You can then keep necessary fonts in the Fonts folder and keep the balance of your fonts elsewhere. When you need to activate a font, turn it on with the font-management software and it's ready to use.

TrueType and Open Type fonts simply work without the need for a helper application. Their format is understood by both Macintosh and Windows operating systems. PostScript fonts require that you use a font rasterizer, such as ATM. This links the bitmapped screen font to the outline printer font and gives you a smooth display. In addition, PostScript fonts must have the screen font in the same folder as the printer font when downloading to the printer.

How you file your fonts is a personal decision. Some file their fonts by type (kind) — keeping Script, Decorative, Serif, Sans-serif, Grunge and Pi fonts in separate folders. The problem with filing in this manner is that you have to decide in what category you would classify each typeface in order to file it.

How would you class these typefaces? Is Broadway Sans Serif or Decorative? Is Optima Serif or Sans Serif? Would you class Poetica Chancery as Script or Decorative?

Others find that a simple alphabetic filing system works best for them. Still, even with this simple filing system, questions may arise. Some are absolute literalists — they would file New Baskerville and New Century Schoolbook under "N." Using this logic, all ITC fonts would be filed under "I." In fact, they should be filed with the rest of the Baskervilles and Centurys, for greatest practicality.

~A/B Screen Fonts	Cascade Script
~C/D Screen Fonts	Caslon
~E/F Screen Fonts	Caslon (Adobe)
~G/H Screen Fonts	Caslon 224
~I/J Screen Fonts	Caslon Book (BE)
~K/L Screen Fonts	Castellar
~M/N Screen Fonts	Catull
~O/P Screen Fonts	Caxton
~Q/R Screen Fonts	Centaur
~S Screen Fonts	Centennial
~T Screen Fonts	Century (ITC)
~U/V Screen Fonts	Century Cond (ITC)
~W/X/Y/Z Screen Fonts	Century Expanded
	Century Oldstyle
	Century Schoolbook (New)
	Cerigo

We group our fonts alphabetically, and then file individually by font family. Note that there are four varieties of Caslon and five varieties of Century.

Some prefer to put all the fonts in an alphabetic range in a single folder. This works reasonably well depending upon how often you need to access the fonts and the number of fonts used. While fonts from different foundries can be mixed, it is best to leave PostScript and TrueType fonts in separate folders.

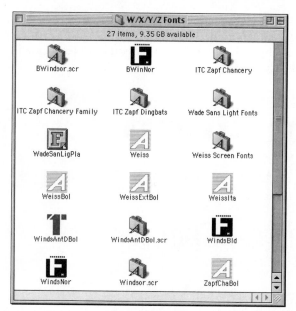

Printer and Screen fonts from several vendors reside in this font folder.

Remember, there is no best way to manage the fonts on your computer, except the way that works best for you. Experiment with different methods and even different font-management software, and then create a custom solution that meets your needs.

Managing Fonts for Printing

For the sake of argument, we will assume that your printing will be done using a Post-Script imaging device, since most quality jobs are printed using PostScript technology. Whether you work with PostScript or TrueType fonts, the font information must be sent to the printer. The information resides in the printer's RAM. TrueType font data is converted to PostScript data. When the job is completed, all fonts used are flushed from the printer's memory, except those that shipped with the printer. They still exist in the printer's ROM.

If both Type 1 PostScript fonts and TrueType fonts having the same name are in the data stream, there is a possibility of error. If their font metrics are not identical, lines of type may fall differently when the job is printed than they did on the screen. This is due, for the most part, to the differing hierarchies of the monitor and the printer.

DISPLAY	PRINTER
Bitmap screen font correct size	Font in Printer's ROM
TrueType font	Font in Printer's RAM
PostScript font rasterized by ATM	Font in attached hard disk
Closest size bitmap screen font	PostScript font
	TrueType font
	Bitmap screen font

As this chart shows, the display, with TrueType native, looks for font information that is almost exactly the opposite of what the printer seeks with PostScript native.

If you are working with PostScript fonts, remember that you need to have both the bitmap screen font and the vector printer font to view the image properly and print it. If you do not have the printer font, the bitmap font is simply resized and printed.

When only a screen font is available, the screen font is resized and printed. This 48-pt. Trump Medieval certainly is unattractive as printed.

Taking a reasonable amount of time to check your system will help you avoid problems when you print. Be sure to check your Fonts folder whenever you install new software. Often new programs will arbitrarily place new fonts on your system. In many cases, these new typefaces will have TrueType and Type 1 fonts packaged together. If you are using primarily TrueType fonts, remove the Type 1 fonts. If you are using primarily PostScript fonts, remove the TrueType. This ensures that what you see on the screen closely resembles what prints.

Font-Related Printing Problems

From time to time a file does not print and returns a PostScript error. Some of these errors are related to fonts and others are not. We will discuss the most common and the means of troubleshooting them.

To find the PostScript error message:

- Watch the Print Monitor.

- Watch the Print dialog box.

- Use an *error handler*, a utility that describes the error and creates a log.

Printing Tricks

The solution for solving most printing problems is the set we call "Printing Tricks". You will note that we refer to them often in the troubleshooting steps.

- Turn the printer off, then on again.

- Select the correct printer.

- Ensure that the correct PPD (PostScript Printer Description File) is chosen.

- Turn Unlimited Downloadable Fonts on, if that option is available.

- Turn off other printer effects in the Setup dialog box.

- Ensure that the settings are correct for both the printer and the document.

VMError

The document needs more printer memory than you have.

- Try Printing Tricks. Does it print now?

- Print with low-resolution graphics or without graphics. Does it print now?
    - If Yes, one or more graphics are consuming the printer's memory. Suppress or delete a graphic, or simplify the problem graphic.
    - If No, the paper size may be too large, too large a print area may be selected or too many fonts are being downloaded. Reduce the paper size, tile the pages or reduce the number of downloadable fonts.

Nostringval or Typecheck

This is caused by a corrupt font, usually a corrupt PostScript printer font. As is the case with files, fonts can become corrupted for no apparent reason.

- Identify which font by elimination. Create a Fonts Disabled folder and place the fonts in this folder, adding them back in until the error occurs again.

- Replace the printer font from your original CD.

LimitCheck

The graphic is too complex to process. There are three possible secondary messages:

- Clip: there is a complex clipping path or mask.
    - Simplify the graphic in its original program by increasing the flatness value or simplifying the mask elements, then resave and reimport.
    - Convert nonrectangular shapes in the page-layout program to a simpler polygon.
    - If a large portion of the graphic is being cropped by the page-layout program, resave the graphic in the original program without the unnecessary area.

- Image or Color Image: TIFF and bitmapped graphics are too complex.
  - Simplify the page, if possible.
  - Increase the printer's resolution.
  - Decrease the graphic's resolution.
- Stroke or Fill: the graphics' paths are too complex for the printer.
  - Increase the flatness values for strokes.
  - Split long paths.

RangeCheck/SetPageParam

Incorrect dimensions have been used for page width, gap and offset. The sum of the three (including page marks) cannot exceed the page-width specifications of the printer.

- Try Printing Tricks. Does it print now?

- Call Tech Support for the imagesetter.

Dicstack Overflow

There is a PostScript problem with a graphic, usually a conflict between an EPS file and the *PostScript dictionary* (yet another dictionary that works behind the scenes).

- Print in Rough mode. Does it print now?

- If Yes, resave the EPS file in the original program and reimport it. Does it print now?

- If No to either question, call Tech Support for the graphics program.

–8133 (Macintosh Only)

This generic postscript error message is preceded by the actual error.

- Try Printing Tricks. Does it print now?

- Watch the Print Monitor to view the exact error. If background printing is off, watch for the error in the Print Status dialog box or use an error handler for a printed copy of the error.

Undefined Offending Command: [various]

This is one of the most frustrating errors. Because the solution is somewhat convoluted, we will show it in chart form.

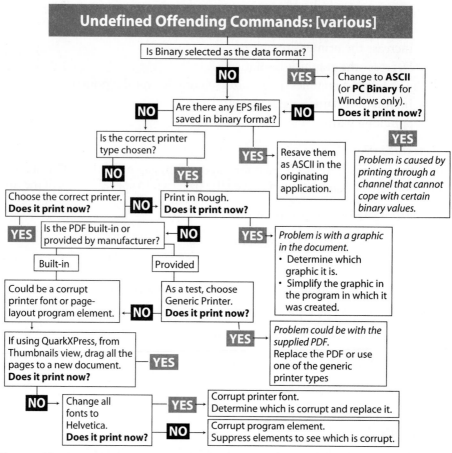

Undefined Offending Commands: [various]

Is Binary selected as the data format?
- NO
- YES → Change to **ASCII** (or **PC Binary** for Windows only). **Does it print now?**
  - NO
  - YES → Problem is caused by printing through a channel that cannot cope with certain binary values.

Are there any EPS files saved in binary format?
- NO
- YES → Resave them as ASCII in the originating application.

Is the correct printer type chosen?
- NO → Choose the correct printer. **Does it print now?**
  - YES
  - NO →
- YES → Print in Rough. **Does it print now?**
  - NO
  - YES → Problem is with a graphic in the document.
    - Determine which graphic it is.
    - Simplify the graphic in the program in which it was created.

Is the PDF built-in or provided by manufacturer?
- Built-in → Could be a corrupt printer font or page-layout program element.
  - If using QuarkXPress, from Thumbnails view, drag all the pages to a new document. **Does it print now?**
    - YES
    - NO → Change all fonts to Helvetica. **Does it print now?**
      - YES → Corrupt printer font. Determine which is corrupt and replace it.
      - NO → Corrupt program element. Suppress elements to see which is corrupt.
- Provided → As a test, choose Generic Printer. **Does it print now?**
  - NO
  - YES → Problem could be with the supplied PDF. Replace the PDF or use one of the generic printer types

While troubleshooting files is an exacting and sometimes painful process, it will reveal what the problem is and determine what you can do to solve the problem.

When preparing a file to take to a service provider, be sure to use your page layout program's utility. This collects fonts and graphics with the document. It often prepares a detailed report, including a listing of colors, styles, graphics and fonts used in the document.

Summary

Taking control of your type is necessary to ensure that your work will print or display as you wish. When you understand the makeup of typefaces, you are somewhat further ahead when problems arise and you need to come up with a solution. In this chapter, you have explored the makeup of fonts, considered how font matching is accomplished and learned how to manage fonts on your computer and in the print stream.

Last Thoughts

Now that you have finished reading all eight chapters, you realize there is much more to type, and to typography, than meets the eye. Hidden beneath the graceful glyphs are invisible design elements, pages of code, and centuries of history and tradition. If you have applied yourself to the material, you have likely become enriched by type lore.

As you meandered through the history and foundations of type in Section 1, you probably developed a sense of language, both spoken and written, and of events — particularly in Europe and the Middle East. Perhaps you aroused in yourself a desire to explore related histories or to examine some of the items mentioned, either in publications or through trips to museums.

You learned that type is a living, growing, evolving entity. Type designed for use on today's presses or on the Internet is technology-based, while retaining the character and ease-of-reading that has been built into type for centuries. While learning this, you also learned how to analyze letterforms, becoming able to identify parts of letters, to measure type horizontally and vertically, and to specify type. You learned some differences between type on Macintoshes and on Windows computers.

You also learned how to categorize type using the Lawson system, and were exposed to a number of typefaces and designers. Through your exploration of type categories, you gained some historic perspectives, as well. You also became familiar with non-standard character sets, and learned the value of using them to improve the look of your documents.

As you became better acquainted with typography in Section 2, you learned that creating readable type includes a maze of details. You learned to consider weight, case, and style when selecting type. You also learned that behind-the-scenes elements of a typeface, such as the Left Sidebearing and built-in kerning, affect the ways that characters interact with each other and with the natural margins for text. You learned how to identify and compensate for bad typography that is a result of the design of the typeface.

You also learned to work with leading and line length to enhance the look of type on the page and readability. These factors influence the color of type, and you discovered the importance of paying attention to details, such as justification, the raggedness of lines and kerning and tracking to ensure an even color throughout the page.

You learned a variety of ways to control type within documents, taking advantage of the automation features of publishing programs. You learned about setting up hyphenation and justification parameters, and how to manage horizontal and vertical alignment. You learned how to control paragraph formatting to avoid stranded lines of type, and you were introduced to styles and their interactivity.

You learned how to handle various real-world challenges from matching type to the message to working with display and text type. In the process you learned that, while there are guidelines, hard-and-fast rules can seldom be applied. You learned about a variety of design methods and devices. You also reviewed some issues with the use of color in type and in design overall.

The challenges of type are not limited to print, as you discovered in our discussion of type and the Internet. You learned about Microsoft's free Core Fonts for the Web, installed on most Windows computers. You also learned how to specify type, and discovered that future versions of HTML will not allow the current method of specifying a typeface. As a result, Cascading Style Sheets (CSS) become extremely important. You also discovered that it is possible to embed fonts in documents, so you don't have to worry about whether or not the reader has the font with which you have designed the page.

A final challenge to all is the mechanics of type. Whether PostScript Type 1, TrueType or Open Type fonts are used, we must manage the fonts on our computers and in the print stream.

You learned about some of the inner workings of fonts — necessary elements of code that are important to font designers, but that function behind the scenes, so those of us who use fonts are basically unaware of them. You also discovered how font matching works under Windows and on the Macintosh — what happens when a font is missing. You even learned how to troubleshoot documents that won't print — what steps you can take to discover what the problem is and to make needed corrections.

We hope this book has given you some insights into type, and that it spurs you to go beyond the basics and to learn more about the aspects of type and typography that interest you most. Perhaps you'll want to learn more about designing with type °or about designing fonts. Alternately, you may wish to delve deeper into techniques of applying type to publications, or embedding fonts in Web pages. Whatever your interest is, we hope you'll continue in it and experience, as we have, the joys of type.

SECTION 4

GALLERY & REFERENCE

The most touching epitaph I ever encountered was on the tombstone of the printer in Edinburgh. It said simply "He kept down the cost and set the type right."

—GREGORY NUNN

Gallery

In Section 1, you gained an historical perspective of type and typography and learned how to identify both parts of a letter and characteristics of primary type categories. Section 2 moved you away from the physical aspects of the characters and toward techniques for creating attractive and effective documents, with emphasis on controlling type on the page both manually and automatically. In Section 3, you explored the challenges that face designers and technicians who use type in the real world.

Our gallery offers a number of color examples that illustrate the concepts and ideas we have presented throughout the book. You will see a number of examples of "breaking the rules," and note that rule-breaking can be effective. The examples here were created by artists and designers from around the United States, and represent typical applications of typography in the commercial world.

FRACTURED FRACTUR

Creator: Robin B. McAllister
Type: Fractur

Turn the page upside-down and you'll still be able to read the word created using the font Fractur as its basis. This application of type as freeform letters — is known as "inversion," a form of ambigram. An inversion can be read rightside-up or upside-down, although the letterform may be substantially different. It is different from a palindrome, which is a word that reads the same way backward or forward, although, as in this case, it may also be a palindrome. While some are easy to create, such as the word SWIMS, others, such as the example above, require the artist to make adjustments to the letterform being used as the basis of the inversion.

NEON SIGNAGE

Creator: Bill Morse
Client: Art & Frame Direct, Inc.
Type: Futura

Applying a neon-like glow to signage can give it a dramatic effect. In this case, the type is also curved to sit on a text path. Notice how care must be taken with letterspace so that not the actual space between letters, but the visual space remains consistent. When working with type curved to fit a path, it is also important to select type that will present well. It should not have distracting elements that will conflict with the smooth transition between letters.

ULTRA FIGURA LOGO

Agency: Leopard, Inc.
Creative Director: Kim Wik
Client: FSI Nutrition
Type: Romeo, Helvetica Heavy

The flowing lines of the artwork in this logo are set at counterpoint by the very angular triangle, which further defines the woman's shape. Nicely complementing the artwork, the typeface selected, Romeo, combines flowing lines with sharp angles. The overall feel of the logo is that use of this dietary supplement will result in a better-looking body.

WOMEN'S HOSPITAL LOGO

Agency: Englehart Dicken
Creative Director: Kent Dicken
Client: Women's Hospital of Indianapolis
Type: ITC Isadora, Berkeley

Smooth, flowing lines of the logo, coupled with the elegant script used for "Women's Hospital" make this logo stand out. The statement "We Are Women's Health Care." is made stronger by the insertion of a simple period, making it a declarative statement, rather than merely a slogan.

POWER 1 LOGO

Agency: Englehart Dicken
Creative Director: Kent Dicken
Client: Power 1 Credit Union
Type: Simplex

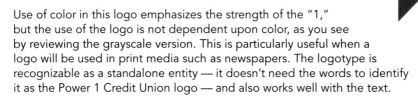

Use of color in this logo emphasizes the strength of the "1," but the use of the logo is not dependent upon color, as you see by reviewing the grayscale version. This is particularly useful when a logo will be used in print media such as newspapers. The logotype is recognizable as a standalone entity — it doesn't need the words to identify it as the Power 1 Credit Union logo — and also works well with the text.

VS LOGO

Creative Director: Bill Morse
Client: Forsman Vintners

This strong typeface, an altered Bodoni, gives strong product identification to this brand of wine. It is designed to suggest the bold taste.

NANO IDENTIFICATION

Creative Director: Bill Morse
Client: Nanothinc
Type: Helvetica

Not just type, but also geometric shapes (and in this case, three-dimensional shapes) go into the creation of a distinctive logotype. The strong geometric look is appropriate to the NANO, which positions itself as the primary resource for nanotechnology.

NANO WORLD

Creative Director: Bill Morse
Client: Nanothinc
Type: Helvetica

Creating a whole-world approach using type effectively portrays NANO's message that nano-technology will soon affect all aspects of life on earth.

Nanothinc is a Web site that positions itself as the "Discovery Channel" for information about nanotechnology — tiny machines the size of molecules.

RACE FOR THE CURE

Agency: Englehart Dicken
Creative Director: Kent Dicken
Client: Women's Hospital of Indianapolis
Type: Poppl Laudatio

Although the text of this ad is light, the message certainly isn't. The powerful headline emphasizes its message by committing the typographic "sin" of mixing type sizes. Rules are made to be broken when there is good cause to break them. Note that, because the headline type is knocking out of the four-color photograph, a sans-serif face with clean, strong lines was selected. In addition, a thin black shadow was added to the type; this both provides definition to the type and acts as a trap to the underlying photo, trengthening the headline type. In addition to the powerful headline, the subhead emphasizes the hospital's commitment to the purpose of the event and salutes the event's organizers and participants.

CENTER FOR HIP & KNEE SURGERY

Agency: Englehart Dicken
Creative Director: Kent Dicken
Client: Kendrick Memorial Hospital
Type: Stone Serif

Two features add to the power of this ad. The first — and most notable — is the wonderful use of white space. White space draws your attention to the important elements of the ad, contributing to their power. The second feature is the creation of the hammock shape by the body text. Even if the text is not read, its message is communicated. The split headline first grabs attention, then leads you to want to read the body copy. The logo and related information at the bottom of the ad is set apart for easy identification.

ART AFFAIR

Agency: Leopard, Inc.
Creative Director: Kim Wik
Client: Contemporary Concepts
Type: ITC Garamond, Helvetica, Citadel Script

Use of the large script "A" carries the reader's attention from the cover to the inside of this well-designed promotion of art. Even though the body text is serif, and reversed out of the background, it holds up well because the background is solid black. Adequate line spacing is employed to enhance the readability of the type. Main points are set in a bold sans-serif face, so they will not be missed.

5-HOUR BREAKFAST SALE

Agency: Leopard, Inc.
Creative Director: Jan Savoie
Client: Élan Contemporary Furnishings
Type: Berkeley, Frutiger, Citadel Script

Elegant typography together with the curving lines of featured contemporary furniture make this invitation inviting. Boldface type accents the features designed to bring preferred customers into the store for the morning event. The open leading makes the invitation easy to read and leads the customer to the main event, which is, after all, the furniture.

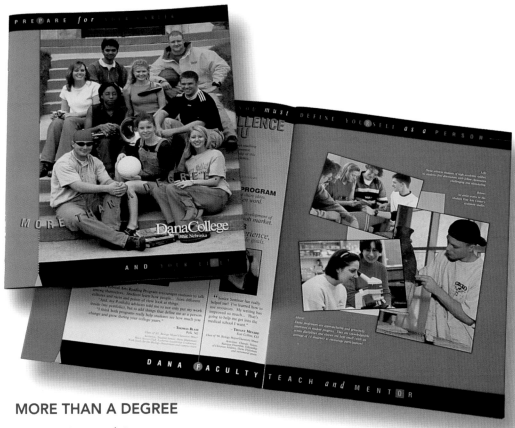

MORE THAN A DEGREE

Agency: Leopard, Inc.
Creative Director: Kim Wik
Client: Dana College
Type: Times New Roman, Helvetica

Vibrant color and vibrant people grace this promotion for Dana College in Blair, Nebraska. Playful type in the headers and footers of each page gives potential students added reason to select the school. "Prepare for your career...and your life," "You must define yourself as a person." The publication is packed with excitement — a wonderful inducement to bring in students who are looking for more than a course schedule, and who want the sense of community that comes with a smaller school.

WAYSIDE INN COOKBOOK

Agency: McAllister & Company
Creative Director: Robin B. McAllister
Client: Longfellow's Wayside Inn
Type: Poetica, Adobe Caslon

This 64-page cookbook features recipes used regularly in America's oldest operating inn, where Longfellow penned the poem "Tales of a Wayside Inn." Contemporary favorites are listed along with foods that Paul Revere may have enjoyed. The cover, section dividers and names of recipes are presented in Poetica, an uncial typeface. The text is set in Adobe Caslon, which was a popular face in Longfellow's day. Dingbats from the Poetica Ornaments font separate recipes when more than one appears on a page. Overall, the cookbook is open and airy — easy to read when preparing meals.

DREAM SEASON

Agency: Leopard, Inc.
Creative Director: Sue Weidner
Client: Opera Omaha
Type: ITC Stone Serif, Stone Sans, Snell Roundhand, Friz Quadrata

If you thought the opera was stodgy, you'd be shaken from that opinion by this tasteful and dramatic presentation. From dreamy purples and soft tints to dramatic earth tones, this brochure grabs your attention and holds it. The type adds to the drama. From body type that softly contrasts with the background to quotes that leap off the page to tout the excellence of the opera company, type is interwoven with the design to extract both emotional and reasoned responses to the brochure's appeal.

ARTISTS WHO CONTRIBUTED WORK TO THIS BOOK:

Kent Dicken
Principal, Creative Director
Englehart Dicken
Indianapolis, Indiana
www.edsads.com

Jan Savoie
Principal, Creative Director
Leopard, Inc.
Omaha, Nebraska
www.leopard-inc.com

Liesel Donaldson
Graphic Designer
Tampa, Florida
www.liesel.com

Sue Weidner
Creative Director
Leopard, Inc.
Omaha, Nebraska
www.leopard-inc.com

Robin McAllister
Principal, McAllister & Company
Bradenton, Florida

Kim Wik
Creative Director
Leopard, Inc.
Omaha, Nebraska
www.leopard-inc.com

Bill Morse
Illustrator
Whitefish Bay, Wisconsin

A big thanks to all of the students from the Art Institute of Ft. Lauderdale who contributed their artwork to this book.

GALLERY

Glossary

Adobe Systems

This San Jose, California-based corporation developed the PostScript language.

Alignment

Horizontal or vertical positioning of the margins of type on a page.

ANSI

American National Standards Institute. The recognized standards-making body for the United States, and the U.S. member of the International Standards Organization (ISO). This organization is responsible for most standards used for audiovisual and computer equipment. On Windows computers, characters are assigned an ANSI control number. The ANSI character set includes characters within the Unicode standard, with the standard keyboard characters falling within the range from 32 to 128.

Antique

Category of type using the DeVinne classification system. Antiques traditionally are single-weight, slab-serif typefaces, but the term is often applied to all slab-serif faces.

Apex

The point at the top of a letter where two strokes meet.

Arm

A horizontal or upward diagonal stroke, attached to the letter at one end and unattached at the other.

Ascender

The part of a lower-case letter that extends above the x-height. In many lettering styles, the ascender is taller than the capital letter.

Ascender Height

The height of a b, d, f, h, k, l or t, measured from the baseline to the top of the letter.

ASCII

American Standard Code for Information Interchange. On Macintosh and other non-Windows computers, characters are assigned an ASCII control number. The ASCII character set includes 256 characters or control codes, with the standard keyboard characters falling within the range from 32 to 128. The upper set of characters (129–256) will not always display or print consistently from font to font.

ATM (Adobe Type Manager)

This utility links PostScript screen fonts with their printer fonts, so they can be viewed accurately on-screen. An expanded version of ATM allows the user to manage fonts, opening and closing individual fonts or sets of fonts without having to reboot the computer.

Attribute

Distinguishing characteristic of the appearance of text. In Cascading Style Sheets, an HTML attribute.

Background

The area behind type or graphics. In order to display type so it will be most readable, there should be sufficient contrast between the color of the background and the color of the type.

Bar

A horizontal stroke linking two strokes of a letter

Baseline

This reference line is used to specify the desired vertical position where characters rest when printed on the same line. Rounded letters will usually dip below the baseline.

Baseline Grid

This grid, when turned on, forces type to align to the grid, irrespective of the leading defined by the paragraph.

Blackletter

This primary type classification closely imitates the brush and pen strokes made by scribes, who drew letters by hand. Heavy Germanic-looking faces, Old English, and uncial hands are included.

Block Books

These small religious books were printed from engraved blocks of wood, which we would call "woodcuts" today.

Body Clearance Line

A small amount of space above the ascender or cap-height line (whichever is taller) built in for clearance between characters when the type is set on a line spacing equal to its size in points.

Body Type

A particular font, usually smaller than 14 point, used for the main text of a printed piece, as opposed to headline (display) type or caption type.

Bold

One of the primary weights of type.

Bold Italic

The italic style of a typeface, combined with the bold weight.

Boolean Operative

A Boolean operative is a mathematical expression in which each of the operands and the result take one of two values.

Bowl

A stroke surrounding a counter.

Bracket

Also called a "fillet," this curved or sloping shape joins the serif to the stem or stroke.

Browser

A software program which interfaces a computer to the World Wide Web. It usually includes a hypertext interpreter and enables viewing of sites and navigation between nodes and sites.

Bulleted List

A list of items preceded by a symbol, rather than a number or letter. The standard bullet is the • figure, but other symbols, such as 3 are often used.

Callout

Type taken from the text and displayed in a larger size to emphasize a point.

Cap Height

The height of a capital letter, measured from the baseline to the top of the letter.

Carding

The process of adding space between paragraphs to achieve vertical justification.

Cascading Style Sheets (CSS)

Style sheets used on the World Wide Web that are applied in a hierarchical order. In order for CSS to work, the browser must be CSS-enabled.

Centered

A justification routine that aligns the centers of lines of type instead of their left or right margins. Sometimes called "Ragged Both" or "Quad Center."

Chancery

A subset of the blackletter classification of type. Chancery type is representative of the flowing style of lettering used by scribes.

Character Bounding Box

Space taken up by the width and height of the letter with no allowance for spacing.

Character Count

Number of characters per a given linear measure, usually in characters per pica (cpp).

Character Origin

A point to the left of the character's bounding box that marks the starting point of a letter. This adds space around the character to avoid the problem of letters crashing into one another.

Character Set

The collection of letters in a given font. In a standard font, this will include the capital and miniscules, numbers and an assortment of non alpha numeric characters. Expert character sets may contain small capitals, fractions, ligatures and oldstyle numbers. The characters, taken collectively, in a non alpha-numeric font, such as Zapf Dingbats, also comprise a character set.

Character Width

The entire width programmed into the character, including its character space. The space between the character origin and the next character point.

Chase

Metal frame for preparing and holding letterpress forms in which metal type and engravings are locked into position to make up a page for reproduction in a relief type of printing press.

Clarendons

Slab-serif typefaces with varying weights, introduced in the mid-19th century.

Class

Method of specifying a group of tags using CSS.

Codex

The Greeks and Romans used small wax tablets for brief documents of a non-permanent nature. Small boards with narrow frames were overlaid with a thin coating of black wax, into which letters were scratched with a stylus, allowing the lighter-colored wood to show through. The tablets could be bound together with thongs or metal rings; a group of tablets bound together was called a "codex."

Color

In typography, the overall grayness of a block or page of type. Type properly set will have a consistent density. Generally, the combination of hue, saturation and value that places a tone on the spectrum.

Complementary Colors

Colors opposite one another on a color wheel.

Columns

Vertical divisions of a page.

Connotation

The set of ideas or meanings associated with a word or suggested by it.

Copyfitting

The art and science of determining the relationship between size and leading of type and the area into which it will be fit.

Corruption

This occurs when, for no apparent reason, a program or a font fails to perform correctly. The solution to this problem is to reinstall the program or font from the original disk.

Counter

An area entirely enclosed by a bowl or crossbar.

CPP

Characters per pica, used to copyfit text.

Crossbar

A horizontal stroke that crosses another stroke.

Cursive

Script or flowing, connected letters.

Decimal Tab

A setting which, when the Tab key is pressed, will align characters to a decimal point.

Declaration

When specifying type for the Web, a property and corresponding value. In the declaration color: blue, color is the property and blue is the value.

Decorative/Display Type

Decorative or Display type is best used in larger sizes. These typefaces are meant to be used in headlines and to convey specific meaning — they are not to be used as text fonts.

Denotation

The direct meaning or set of meanings of a word or expression.

Descender

The part of a letter that extends below the baseline.

Descender Height

The distance between the baseline and the lowest point of the descender.

Design Grid

A structured approach to creating documents. The grid divides pages horizontally and vertically.

Diacritical Mark

A mark, point or sign added or attached to a letter to give it a particular phonetic value, such as é, ö or ç.

Dictionary

Part of a computer program or font containing rules for a particular function, such as a hyphenation or spelling dictionary.

Dingbat

Any non alpha numeric character; also called a "pi" character.

Discretionary Hyphen

A hyphenation point or points that will allow the word to be broken only at the pica of insertion. Discretionary hyphens appear only if the word has been broken.

Display Type

See *Decorative/Display Type*.

DPI

Dots Per Inch. A measure of the resolution of output devices, ranging from laser printers to imagesetters.

Drop Cap

The first character (or characters) of a paragraph, with a baseline a specified number of lines deep and extending to at least the top of the ascenders of the first line of the paragraph.

Ear

A short protrusion of the letter g. Depending on the typeface, it may also be found on the letters p and r.

Egyptian

A group of slab-serif typefaces having a lower case and bracketed serifs.

Electrotyping

A process for making a durable printing plate. In the electrotyping process, type is set and a cast (usually from wax) is made; it is then coated in graphite and placed in an electroplating bath. A copper shell is built up in the shape of the original type.

Em

A measurement of linear space; the unit of measurement is exactly as wide and as high as the point size being set. A 12-point em is exactly 12 points square.

Em Dash

A dash the width of an em, approximately centered on the x-height of characters. Used to separate word groups in the written material.

Em Space

A fixed space (non-justifying) the width of an em.

Embedded Fonts

Fonts that are usable only for viewing specific pages; they are a part of the page, not downloaded to the user's computer.

En Dash

A dash half the width of an em, approximately centered on the x-height of characters. An en dash is used to replace the word "to" or "through." It is used to separate words in a phrase, such as "December 15–January 2." The en dash is also used to represent the minus sign in mathematical expressions.

En Space

A fixed space (non-justifying) half the width of an em.

Encoding Vector

A mini-program contained within fonts that show which characters and character mapping will be used.

Engraved

Engraved fonts have the appearance of having been cut or chiseled into metal or stone.

Error Handler

A program that prints out information about PostScript errors.

Expert Set

A superset of gylphs for some typefaces. The expert set may include small caps, swash characters, ligatures, oldstyle figures, fractions, ornaments and the like.

Eye

The enclosed space in the upper portion of the character e.

Family

All the styles and weights descending from a specific typeface design. The Times family includes Times Roman, Times Italic, Times Semibold, Times Semibold Italic, Times Bold, Times Bold Italic and Times Extrabold.

FamilyName

The identifying name of an entire family of type, such as Stone Sans or Adobe Minion.

Feathering

The process of adding space between lines to achieve vertical justification.

Figure Height

The height, measured from the baseline to the top of the character, of numeric characters.

Fillet

See *Bracket*.

Finial or Terminal

An ending of a serif character other than a serif.

Flatness Value

An attribute used in complex artwork and masking. The lower the flatness, the more tightly curves and detail will be reproduced. Higher flatness numbers decrease the risk of crashing the imaging device.

Flex Space

A fixed (non-justifying) space, the width of which is user-defined, based on percentages of an em or of an en.

Flush Left

A justification routine where the left margin is even and the right margin is unjustified. Also called "Quad Left" and "Ragged Right."

Flush Right

A justification routine where the right margin is even and the left margin is unjustified. Also called "Quad Right" and "Ragged Left."

Folio

Page number.

Font

All the glyphs in a given typeface. Traditionally, one size of a typeface. A PostScript or TrueType font contains all sizes of the typeface.

Font Call

A request in the print stream for a specific typeface to be used.

Font Dictionary

The font dictionary is code contained "inside" the font. Some of the information is accessible using Adobe Type Manager or Microsoft's TTF Properties tool. Some of the information is available only when using advanced developer's tools. To use fonts properly, you don't need to know any of this internal information. The font dictionary includes the following coded information: FontType, FontMatrix, FontName, FontInfo, Encoding, FontBBox, UniqueID, CharStrings.

Font Management

Means of controlling how fonts are used on the computer. Font-management software includes Adobe Type Manager, Suitcase and Font Reserve.

Font Mapping

Designating a replacement font to use if a font is missing. Your replacement font can be permanent or temporary.

Font Matching

Another term for font mapping.

Font Metrics

Information coded into fonts that controls the appearance of such elements as character widths and letterspacing values, and information about ascenders and descenders and kerning pairs built into the font.

FontName

A distinctive identification, which every font must have. The name consists of the FamilyName followed by a hyphen, then style attributes in the same order as the FullName.

Font Rasterizer

A computer program that converts vector images such as fonts into bitmaps so they can be printed.

Font Suitcase

A container into which PostScript screen fonts or TrueType fonts are placed.

Fontinfo Dictionary

An optional subdictionary within the Font Dictionary.

Fonts Folder

The folder in which, unless a type managing utility is used, fonts are placed on the Macintosh and the folder in which TrueType fonts are placed under Windows.

FullName

The entire, unabbreviated font name, complete with attributes. It includes the FamilyName, style, weight and width (if appropriate). The FullName must begin with the correct FamilyName. The weight attribute should be the same as the Weight keyword in the FontInfo dictionary and in the Adobe Font Metric (AFM) file.

Garage Font

Garage or Grunge fonts are typefaces that break all the rules of good typographic design. They are distorted, have erratic baselines and look good in graffiti.

GASP

Graphic Arts Service Provider. Company that performs a variety of high-end services, including scanning, image manipulation and imaging of files at high resolution.

Geometric

A subcategory of sans-serif type, it includes the Futuras and Kabel, among others. These typefaces have a single stroke weight, and clean geometric lines.

Glyph

A single typographic character.

Glyph Scaling

The ability to horizontally or vertically scale typographic characters.

Gothics

Sans-serif typefaces with a single stroke weight.

Grotesque

A subcategory of sans-serif type, it includes typefaces with a variable stroke weight.

Grunge Font

See *Garage Font*.

Gutters

Space between columns of a page. Also called "alleys."

H&J

Hyphenation and Justification. The process by which a page-layout program applies the rules and parameters specified for hyphenating text and allowing proper spacing.

Hierarchy

The order information is presented in, or the importance of the information.

Hinting

A map of the character onto a grid to produce the most pleasing character shape when the type is printed to a low-resolution printer.

HTML

HyperText Markup Language. The coding or tagging method used to format documents for the World Wide Web.

Humanist

This subcategory of sans-serif type includes the Gill, Optima and Frutiger families. There is a variation in stroke weight.

Hyperlink

In pages on the World Wide Web, the primary method of navigating between pages. Hyperlinks contain HTML-coded references that point to other Web pages, to which the browser then advances.

Hyphenation

Separating or joining words using the hyphen character. Hyphenation follows language-specific rules for separating words. A superset of these rules may be made to restrict hyphenation within documents.

Hyphenation Zone

A point in a line of text, measured from the end of the line, within which there must be a hyphenatable point in a word. If a space occurs within the zone, no hyphenation occurs. If there is no hyphenatable point in a word within the zone, the entire word breaks to the next line.

Ideogram

A written symbol that represents an idea or object directly, rather than a particular word or speech sound.

Illuminates

A decorative letter, usually colored, used to enhance the appearance of a document.

Imagesetter

A high-resolution printer. Imagesetters usually print to photographic paper or film.

In-line Graphic

An image placed within the text of a document, that moves with the text stream as though it were a text object.

Instances

Variations of a Multiple Master typeface.

Intercolumnar Space

Space between columns; gutters.

Interline Space

Space between lines; leading.

Internet

A system of computer networks, international in scope, that facilitates data communication services such as remote login, file transfer, electronic mail and newsgroups. The Internet is a means to connect existing computer networks that greatly extends the reach of each participating system.

Internet Explorer

A Web browser from Microsoft.

Interparagraph Space

Space between paragraphs. This includes the leading, plus any additional space above or space below the paragraph specified.

Italic

One of the primary styling options for type. Clicking on Italic will produce the style that has been designed for the font. It is usually not simply an obliqued form of the typeface, but the letterform often differs substantially from the roman, or normal, font.

Justification

Alignment of text, specifying which margin(s) will align. Text may be justified with both margins aligning; flush left and flush right indicate which margin aligns or is "flush"; a centered justification indicates that neither margin aligns, but the text is centered horizontally on the copy area.

Kerning

Adjusting two consecutive letters so the space between them is pleasing to the eye.

Knock Out

The process of eliminating all background colors.

Leading

The space between lines of type, measured from baseline to baseline. The term originated from the compositor's practice of placing thin strips of lead between lines of type in order to space them further apart.

Left Sidebearing

Space built in between the true Character Origin and the beginning of the Character Bounding Box.

Leg

A downward diagonal stroke, attached to the letter at one end and unattached at the other.

Letter Spacing

Space designed between letters; alternately, the alteration of that space that may be inserted using kerning, tracking and H&J routines.

Letterpress

The method of printing in which the image, or ink-bearing areas, of the printing plate are raised above the nonimage areas. When ink is applied to the surface, only the high areas contact the inking mechanism. Paper applied to the raised, inked surfaces under pressure transfer the image.

Line Spacing

See *Leading*.

Link

In letterform, the stroke tying together the upper and lower sections of the letter g. In Internet usage, text containing HTML-coded references to take the browser to another screen or page.

Linotype

A key-operated linesetting and typecasting machine that employed reusable brass matrices; the device cast an entire line of lead type at a time. The Linotype was invented by Ottmar Merganthaler, who founded the Merganthaler Linotype Corporation; it is now a part of Heidelberg Corporation.

Logogram

"Word signs," originally coming from ancient Egypt. Logograms in use today include the ampersand (&), dollar sign ($) and copyright symbol (©), among others.

Logotype

A special ligature, symbol, trademark, emblem, trade name or any other combination of art, characters, words or phrases produced as a single graphic and used to represent the name of a publication, business, company, product or organization.

Loop

The descender of a g when it is entirely enclosed. (When it is not enclosed it is a tail.)

Lowercase

Miniscules, or letters that are not capitalized. Originally called "lowercase" because the type was in the lower portion of a printer's type case.

Majuscule

Capital letters.

Margins

Unprinted space on a page surrounding, beside, above and below text or illustrations.

Miniscule

Lowercase letters.

Misregistration

The inaccurate overlaying of ink from separate plates, causing a blurry or unsusable reproduction.

Modern

One of the primary categories of type. There are often extremes of contrast between thick and thin strokes. The designs began in the late-18th and early-19th centuries.

Monospaced

Typefaces in which each character takes an equal amount of space. Courier is an example of a monospaced type style.

Mosaic

The first Web browser.

Multiline Composition

An H&J routine used by some programs. It references multiple lines of type to achieve the best hyphenation and justification solution, based on the H&J parameters.

Multiple Master

A subset of PostScript font technology. Each typeface includes two or more sets of master designs, which allows for a dynamic range of possible font variations. The weight axis allows a dynamic range from light to bold; width axis, from condensed to extended; style axis, from sans serif to serif; and optical size axis to enhance readability at any size.

Neo-Grotesque

A subset of the sans-serif type classification. Neo-Grotesques include the Helvetica and Univers families of type.

Netscape Navigator

A Web browser.

Next Character Origin

Space to the right of a character's bounding box; it builds in space around the character.

Nib

The portion of a pen with which ink is applied to the substrate. The shape and angle of the nib, coupled with the angle at which the pen is held, determine the form of the lettering style.

Nonbreaking Character

Usually a hyphen. The letters preceding and following the character are forced to remain on the same line. A reasonable use for a nonbreaking character might be the word "A-line."

Nonbreaking Space

A space programmed to disallow a word break. The word immediately prior to and immediately following the nonbreaking space are forced to remain on the same line. A reasonable use for a nonbreaking space might be "St. Louis."

Numbered List

A list wherein each item begins with a number.

Oblique

To slant a letter or an object at any angle. Some italic letters are called "oblique" even though they are designed as italic letters.

Offset Lithography

A member of the planographic classification of printing. It utilizes the principle that oil (ink) and water do not mix. Image areas on printing plates are treated to accept ink and non-image areas are treated to accept water. The image on the plate prints onto an intermediate rubber blanket cylinder whch transfers (offsets) the image to the substrate.

Oldstyle

This primary category of type began with the first roman face, designed by Nicholas Jensen in 1470 and with the first italic, designed by Aldus Manutius in 1471. Oldstyle typefaces have a relatively consistent stroke weight. The stress is slightly inclined to the left. Early Oldstyle typefaces exhibit a diagonal crossbar on the lowercase e and an ascender height similar to that of capital letters. In later Oldstyles this stroke is usually horizontal and the ascenders are taller than the capitals.

On-Demand Printing

A method of producing only the required number of documents at a given time using electronically stored information.

Open Type

Type format developed jointly by Adobe and Microsoft, it is a superset of both TrueType and Type 1 fonts. These fonts facilitate the handling of large character sets using Unicode encoding, which allows for better international support and support for more typographic glyphs, such as ligatures and oldstyle characters. In addition, the digital signatures carried by Open Type fonts allow operating systems and browsers to identify the source and integrity of the font file, including fonts embedded in Web documents.

Ornament

A decorative glyph.

Orphan

An orphan occurs when the first line of a paragraph falls at the bottom of a column or page.

Outdent

A hanging indent. The first line of the paragraph extends further to the left than the succeeding lines.

Overprint

To print over an area that has already been printed.

PANOSE Typeface Matching System

A numeric classification of fonts according to visual characteristics, intended to substitute fonts of similar appearance.

Papyrus

A parchment-like paper made from the pith, or inner portion of the stalk, of the papyrus plant. The pith was cut into thin strips, pressed together and dried to form a smooth, thin writing surface.

Parchment

An early substrate, made from the skins of sheep and goats. It replaced papyrus as a writing material.

Pi

Type that is not part of the character set of the font, and is generally a symbol character. Since these characters were not part of standard font sets, they were considered to be jumbled, disarranged or mixed. Early Linotype machines included a Pi chute which delivered these nonstandard characters for manual filing.

Pi Font

A font made up entirely of pi characters.

Pica

Unit of measure. Twelve points. A PostScript pica is 1/6 of an inch, but traditionally, 6 picas equals 0.996264 inch.

Pixelation

The tendency for oblique characters to develop "jaggies" on screen and for fine lines to either become clunky or to disappear, due to the low resolution of monitors.

Point

Unit of measure. In PostScript, $\frac{1}{72}$™ inch, but traditionally 0.01387 inch. The original point system, the Didot, had exactly 72 points to the inch — the French Imperial inch, which was longer than the English inch, and went away (along with the Imperial heads) in the French Revolution. The traditional American point system was established by the United States Typefounders Association in 1886. The point was set to be $\frac{1}{12}$™ of a pica. An 830 pica (996 point) length was defined as equal to 35 centimeters.

Point Size

The size of a typeface. The point size is measured from the descender to the top of the body clearance line.

PostScript

A computer language invented by Adobe Systems, Inc. of San Jose, California, that is used to define the appearance of type and images on the printed page. A method of communicating between computers and outut divices.

Postscript Font

A font utilizing the PostScript language, and comprised of two distinct parts: the printer font, which is an outline and is ultimately stored in the output device, and the screen font, which is a bitmap and is stored in the workstation. Both parts of the font must be resident on the system to print a document containing a PostScript font. PostScript fonts are hinted for low resolution printing. Also called "Type 1" fonts.

Postscript Interpreter

Computer program that processes a PostScript page file for printout.

PPI

Pixels Per Inch. Used for monitor and scanner resolutions.

Printer

Any device that will create a physical image of a digital file. In the graphic arts, most printers use the PostScript language. Printers include laser printers, film recorders, imagesetters, platemakers, xerographic, injet, wax and dye sublimation printers, even presses.

Printer Driver

A program that interprets the program data, providing the commands and signals required by the printer.

Printer Font

The part of the PostScript font system that is stored in or downloaded to the printout device.

Property

A stylistic parameter that can be influenced through CSS. This specification defines a list of property names and their corresponding values. In the declaration color: blue, color is the property and blue is the value.

Pull Quote

See *Callout*.

Ragged Text

Text that has been set with one or both margins unjustified (not flush). The advantage of tagged text is that the space between each word is consistent, allowing the eye to flow smoothly across the line.

Raised Caps

A technique, sometimes used for the first paragraph of an article, where the first character of the paragraph is larger than the rest of the letters, with the baseline resting on the baseline of the first line of type in the paragraph.

Relief Printing

A printing process that uses a metal, rubber or photopolymer printing plate on which the image areas are raised above the non-image areas.

Right-Aligning Tab

A setting which, when the Tab key is pressed, will align the right edges of the text to a specified position.

RIP (Raster Image Processor)

The part of an output device that rasterizes information so that it may be imaged by a printer.

River

Wide areas of white running through a column of type, caused by poor hyphenation and justification routines.

Roman

One of the primary styling options for type. It is generally the base font, such as Times Roman. Alternately, an all-encompassing term for serif typefaces.

Rule

A printed line. In CSS, a declaration and its selector.

Running Foot

Information or a title that is repeated at the bottom of each page or a series of pages. They may, or may not, contain folios.

Running Head

Information or a title that is repeated at the top of each page or a series of pages. They may, or may not, contain folios.

Sans Serif

A primary category of type, meaning without (sans) serifs. Strokes tend to be similar in width, though the Neo-Grotesque and Humanist type styles display some contrast. The italics of many Sans Serif typefaces are, in fact, obliques rather than true italics, which experience a change in the shape of some letters.

Screen

When speaking of hardware, the monitor. Also, a process of applying a tint to an image.

Screen Font

The part of the PostScript font system that is stored in the workstation. Screen fonts may be shared with others.

Script, Cursive And Brush

A primary category of type, using the Lawson system. The category includes any connecting or nonconnecting style that appears to have been created with a pen or brush. These letters can be very delicate or very bold, formal or informal.

Scriptorium

In the Middle Ages, a large workroom in monasteries where manuscripts were copied.

Scroll

Sheets of papyrus glued together, side to side, to form a roll 5–12 inches wide and 15–40 feet long, with writing on only one side. The scroll was called a "volumen"; its papyrus was rolled around a brightly painted, gilded stick with knobs at both ends, called an "umbilicus." The scroll was held in the right hand and unrolled, column by column, onto the roller held in the left hand. When the reader reached the end of the roll or had read enough, the roll was rewound onto the umbilicus.

Selector

A string that identifies what elements the corresponding rule applies to.

Sentence Case

A headline style wherein only the first word and any proper nouns are capitalized.

Serif

A beginning or finishing line drawn at a right angle or an oblique angle to the stem or stroke. The word comes from the Dutch *shreef*, which means line. Also, a typeface having serifs.

Service Bureau

See *GASP*.

Set Solid

Lines of type set with leading identical to the point size. 10 point type set on 10 points of leading is set solid.

SGML

Standard Generalized Markup Language. A markup language for representing documents on computers. HTML is based on SGML.

Shoulder

A rounded portion of a lowercase letter that connects two vertical stems or strokes.

Skew

To distort the appearance of an image.

Slab Serif

A primary category of type. Slab-Serif typefaces generally exhibit a vertical stress. While there is some variation in the stroke weight of many faces, it is very nearly consistent throughout each letterform. Serifs are very heavy — sometimes the same weight as the primary stroke of the character.

Slug

A strip of metal produced by a hot metal typesetting machine containing a line of characters.

Small Caps

Capital letters that are approximately the same height as lowercase letters. Although small caps can be manufactured by simply reducing the point size of the capital letter, small caps that are designed for a font are preferred. Manufactured small caps. Designed small caps.

Spell-check

A tool available in some computer programs that checks the spelling of words against a dictionary, rules and algorithms. It is not a substitute for a proofreader.

Spine

The primary curve in the letter S.

Spur

A short, pointed projection from a stem or stroke, such as may be found on a C, G or t, depending on the design of the typeface.

Standard Font

A font containing uppercase and lowercase letters, numbers and a selection of symbol characters, as opposed to containing small caps, oldstyle numbers, swash characters or pi characters.

Stem

The primary vertical stroke of a character, not including decorations such as serifs or stroke endings.

Stereotyping

A process for making a durable printing plate. Stereotyping begins by making a mold of the type using a heat-resistant papier-mâché. Molten metal is then poured into the mold to create the cast plate.

Stress

The angle of a curved stroke, which implies the stroke of a pen, if the letter were to be created by a pen which creates thick and thin strokes.

Style Sheet

A collection of character attributes and paragraph formats that can be applied in one step to a paragraph or to a range of characters. Collectively, all the styles in a document, and their interactivity with one another.

Styled Type

Type that is given its bold, italic and bold italic attributes by clicking on those attributes in a menu, as opposed to selecting the typeface from a menu. The practice is undesirable because, in larger font families, the bold of a font may not exist, or it may be a bold weight that is not desired.

Swash

A flourished terminal, stem or stroke added to a character.

Syllabary

A list of symbols, each of which represents a syllable.

Symbol Font

Any font made up of nonalphanumeric glyphs.

Tag

On the Web, a term used to describe the commands or instructions associated with HTML or Web-page code.

Tail

An extension projecting downward from a letter and usually falling below the baseline, attached at one end and unattached at the other.

Terminal

See *Finial.*

Thin Space

A fixed (non-justifying) space one half the width of an en space.

Tracking

Control of overall letterspace.

Transitional

A primary category of type. This stage of type development was begun near the end of the 17th century. These fonts are transitional between fonts having the relatively consistent stroke weight with strongly bracketed serifs and those having contrasting stroke weights with unbracketed serifs (the Modern category). Transitional type features greater contrast between stroke weights and sharp, straight serifs. The stress of curved strokes is nearly vertical.

TrueType

An outline font format created by Apple Computer and enhanced by Microsoft Corporation. This is a one-part font that acts as both screen and printer font. TrueType fonts are hinted for low-resolution printing.

Type On A Path

Type that is attached to a vector path.

Type Style

The form of a type face, such as italic, roman, condensed, extended or engraved.

Type Weight

The boldness of a type face. Standard weights include ultra light, thin, light, regular, medium, semi (demi) bold, bold, heavy and black.

Typesetters

Devices used to mechanically prepare type for the printing process. First generation typesetters prepared type for relief printing. Second generation typesetters used device-dependent glass, plastic and film masters. Light was flashed through the master onto photosensitive material, which was then developed and printed to a printing plate. Third generation typesetters used font data generated from a cathode-ray tube or laser character generator and "drawn" onto the photosensitive material. Fourth generation typesetters, or imagesetters, used electronically stored font data, but they have the added ability to combine line art and halftones with the type (a completely composed page).

Typography

The arrangement, style and general appearance of matter printed from type. It is the application of art to the science of type.

Uncial

A form of majuscule writing having a curved or rounded shape, and used in about the 3rd to the 9th century CE.

Uppercase

Capital letters. In the days of metal type, capital letters were stor7ed in the upper portion of a printer's typecase.

Value

Together with a property, comprises a CSS declaration. In the declaration color: blue, color is the property and blue is the value.

Variable Spacing

As opposed to monospaced, Typefaces in which each character is assigned a specific width. Most typefaces today use variable spacing.

Vellum

Made from calfskin, this writing material was used for special copies of books. Vellum and parchment were made by carefully washing the skins, then covering them with lime to loosen the hair. When the hair was removed, the skin was stretched on a frame, scraped, dusted with sifted chalk and polished with pumice. Parchment and vellum were used as early as the 5th century BCE; they gradually replaced papyrus, beginning about 100 CE, and virtually displacing papyrus by the middle of the 5th century as the standard material for a book or codex.

Vertex

The point where two strokes meet near the baseline of a letter.

Vertical Justification

The process of adjusting the interline and interparagraph spacing so that top and bottom lines of all pages fall at the same point.

W3C

World Wide Web Consortium. The consortium develops interoperable technologies (specifications, guidelines, software and tools) to lead the Web to its full potential as a forum for information, commerce, communication and collective understanding.

Websafe Colors

216 colors that display correctly on both Windows and Macintosh computers.

Widow

The last line of a paragraph that falls at the top of a column. Also, the last line of a paragraph consisting of only one word.

Widow And Orphan Control

Routines contained in H&J parameters that force the a specified number of lines in a paragraph to stay together. Also called "Keeps" parameters.

Woodcuts

Illustrations cut in relief into wood blocks, for the purpose of printing the image.

Word Spacing

Space between words as defined by the designer of the typeface, or as specified in H&J parameters.

Word Widows

The last line of a paragraph that consists of only one word.

World Wide Web

It has been described as "the universe of network-accessible information; an embodiment of human knowledge." It is a collection of pages that have a user-friendly graphic interface and contain text, images and hypertext links.

Wraparounds

The process of causing type to wrap around a graphic. The type's distance from the edges of the graphic or its bounding box are specified in the wraparound parameter.

WYSIWYG

"What You See Is What You Get" impression conveyed by monitors. Because of the difference in resolution between monitors and output devices, this is merely an illusion.

X-Height

The height of a lower case x, measured from the baseline.

Xylography

The process of printing small religious books called "block books" printed from engraved blocks of wood, which we would call "woodcuts" today.

Index

A

abbreviations 60
accents 29
acronyms 33
aleph 9
aligned 69
aligning pages 96
alignment 69. 89
American/British point system 27
ANSI 31
apex 25
apostrophe 32, 79
Aramaic 9
ARPANET 20
ascender 25, 27
ASCII 31
AtypI system 36
automation features 89
auxiliary dictionary 93

B

bar 25
base 25
basefont 132
baseline 25, 27
beta 9
blackletter 37
bold 16
bold italic 16
bracket 27
browser 131, 132
built-in kerning pairs 76
bulleted lists 85

C

callouts 83, 117, 127
cap height 27, 28
captions 61
cascading style sheets 147, 149
case 60
categories of type 35
character bounding box 63
character count 28
character origin 63
character set 24, 35

chi 9
cicero 27
clarendon 24
clay tables 8
clipping path 126
codex 11
color 58, 72, 135
color of type 72
columns per page 72
composing stick 14
condensed 21
connotation 108
consonants 8
contrast 135
copyright symbol 80
core fonts for the Web 139
counter 26
courier 24, 31
CP/M 18
creating lists 85
crossbar 25
CSS 149

D

daggers 29
data processing 17
De Vinne system 36
decorative alphabets 113
decorative/display 37
default font size 131
delta 9
denotation 108
descender 25
descending letters 25
diagamma 10
didot point system 27
DIN Schriften system 36
direct-to-plate 19
direct-to-press 19
discretionary hyphen 33
display type 107, 113
dots per inch 18
double prime 32
downloadable fonts 21
drop caps 113, 119

E

ellipsis 33
em 28
em dash 80
em dashes 32
em space 81
embedded images 125
en dash 32, 80
en space 81
encoding vector 30
error handler 161
expanded 21
expert character sets 53

F

feathering 97
figures 27
finial 26
flex space 81
flush left 69
flush right 69
fold 134, 135
font dictionary 155
font mapping 156
font matching 156
font metrics 157
font-management 21
fontbbox 155
fontinfo 155
fontmatrix 155
fontname 155
fonts embedded 149
fonts in common use 151
fractions 53
frames 136

G

gamma 9
GASP 31
gimel 9
glass-matrix grids 16
glyph anatomy 24
glyphs 24, 35
graduated tint 125
gutters 71

197

H

h&j 91
headlines 63, 107
hierarchical levels 100
hinting technology 21
horizontal/vertical alignment 96
HTML 20, 130, 136
HTML styles 147
hyphenate 93
hyphenation and justification 91
hyphens 32, 79

I

imagesetters 17
in-line graphic 73
inch 32
inch and foot marks 79
indent 64, 120
international characters 29
Internet 20, 129
interparagraph leading 97
intertype 17
invisible space 62
italic 16, 61, 91

J

justification 58, 69

K

kerning 27, 64, 76, 77, 89
kerning pairs 57
knocked out 123

L

laser character generator 16
Lawson system 36
leading 15, 27, 65, 141
left justified 69
letterforms 24
letterspace 58
ligatures 53
limitcheck 162
line length 58, 67, 72
lines 57, 62, 81
logotypes 122
loop 25
lowercase 10, 29

M

majuscules 10
managing fonts 158
manual adjustments 89
margins and columns 70
measurement of elements 62
measuring type 27, 62
mechanics of type 62
misregistration 75
monospaced 24
multimedia documents 19
Multiple Master fonts 152, 153

N

naming fonts 154
non-breaking space 81
Novarese system 36
NSFNET 20
numbered lists 87

O

OCR 16
offset lithography 16
on-demand printing 19
open type 21, 151, 154, 158
ornamental fonts 30
orphans 99
outlines 21

P

PANOSE 157
paragraph attributes 86
paragraph indents 81
paragraph marks 29
pi 37
pica 27, 28
pictographic 7
point 27
point system 27
PostScript 18, 21, 29, 151
PostScript fonts 18, 152, 158
ppd 162
print and preview embedding 152
print monitor 161, 163
printer font 20, 29, 152
psi 9
pull quotes 72, 84
punctuation 29

Q

quotation marks 78
quotes and related characters 78

R

ragged left/right 69
raised caps 119
registered trademark symbol 80
registration 75
right justified 69
river 69, 95
ROM-based fonts 21
rules 81

S

sans serif 24, 37, 38, 45, 58
screen font 20, 152
screen resolution 133
script 37
sentence case 60
serif 26, 35, 58
skewed 21
slab serif 37
slug 15
small caps 27, 60

space above/before/below 57, 97
spacing options 81
special characters 78, 80, 143
specifying type in html 141
spell-checker 33
spine 25
spots per inch 18
spread 128
stem 25
stress 24
stroke 24
styles 100
subheads 61
supplemental characters 30
symbols 29, 30

T

tab 32
tables 136
thin space 81
three-column grid 71
tracking and kerning 76, 77, 89
tracking tables 76
transitional 37, 40
TrueType
        20, 21, 29, 151, 153, 158
Type 1 fonts 20, 151
Type 1 PostScript 20
type and color 122
type and graphics 123
type in boxes 117
type on a path 125
type on Web pages 129
type size 58
type styles 37
type with rules 57, 81
Typefinder system 36
typographer's quotes 143

U

underlines 91, 136
unnumbered lists 87
uppercase 29

V

variable-data printing 19
vellum 12
vertex 25
vertical justification 97
vmerror 162
Vox system 36

W

Web-safe colors 143
Web-safe palettes 143
weight 58, 59, 155
widows 99
wraparounds 125
WYSIWYG 17

X

x-height 27, 28, 58, 63